PERSEPOLIS

PERSEPOLIS

MARJANE SATRAPI

PANTHEON

Library of Congress Cataloging-in-Publication Data
Satrapi, Marjane, 1969-
[Persepolis. English]
Persepolis / Marjane Satrapi.
    p. cm.
ISBN 0-375-42230-7
1. Satrapi, Marjane, 1969—Comic books, strips, etc. I. Title.
PN6747.S245 P4713 2003   741.5'944—dc21   2002190806

www.pantheonbooks.com
Printed in the United States of America
First American Edition
9 8

INTRODUCTION

In the second millennium B.C., while the Elam nation was developing a civilization alongside Babylon, Indo-European invaders gave their name to the immense Iranian plateau where they settled. The word "Iran" was derived from "Ayryana Vaejo," which means "the origin of the Aryans." These people were semi-nomads whose descendants were the Medes and the Persians. The Medes founded the first Iranian nation in the seventh century B.C.; it was later destroyed by Cyrus the Great. He established what became one of the largest empires of the ancient world, the Persian Empire, in the sixth century B.C. Iran was referred to as Persia — its Greek name — until 1935 when Reza Shah, the father of the last Shah of Iran, asked everyone to call the country Iran.

Iran was rich. Because of its wealth and its geographic location, it invited attacks: From Alexander the Great, from its Arab neighbors to the west, from Turkish and Mongolian conquerors, Iran was often subject to foreign domination. Yet the Persian language and culture withstood these invasions. The invaders assimilated into this strong culture, and in some ways they became Iranians themselves.

In the twentieth century, Iran entered a new phase. Reza Shah decided to modernize and westernize the country, but meanwhile a fresh source of wealth was discovered: oil. And with the oil came another invasion. The West, particularly Great Britain, wielded a strong influence on the Iranian economy. During the Second World War, the British, Soviets, and Americans asked Reza Shah to ally himself with them against Germany. But Reza Shah, who sympathized with the Germans, declared Iran a neutral zone. So the Allies invaded and occupied Iran. Reza Shah was sent into exile and was succeeded by his son, Mohammad Reza Pahlavi, who was known simply as the Shah.

In 1951, Mohammed Mossadeq, then prime minister of Iran, nationalized the oil industry. In retaliation, Great Britain organized an embargo on all exports of oil from Iran. In 1953, the CIA, with the help of British intelligence, organized a coup against him. Mossadeq was overthrown and the Shah, who had earlier escaped from the country, returned to power. The Shah stayed on the throne until 1979, when he fled Iran to escape the Islamic revolution.

Since then, this old and great civilization has been discussed mostly in connection with fundamentalism, fanaticism, and terrorism. As an Iranian who has lived more than half of my life in Iran, I know that this image is far from the truth. This is why writing *Persepolis* was so important to me. I believe that an entire nation should not be judged by the wrongdoings of a few extremists. I also don't want those Iranians who lost their lives in prisons defending freedom, who died in the war against Iraq, who suffered under various repressive regimes, or who were forced to leave their families and flee their homeland to be forgotten.

One can forgive but one should never forget.

Marjane Satrapi
Paris, September 2002

PERSEPOLIS

THE VEIL

THIS IS ME WHEN I WAS 10 YEARS OLD. THIS WAS IN 1980.

AND THIS IS A CLASS PHOTO. I'M SITTING ON THE FAR LEFT SO YOU DON'T SEE ME. FROM LEFT TO RIGHT: GOLNAZ, MAHSHID, NARINE, MINNA.

IN 1979 A REVOLUTION TOOK PLACE. IT WAS LATER CALLED "THE ISLAMIC REVOLUTION".

THEN CAME 1980: THE YEAR IT BECAME OBLIGATORY TO WEAR THE VEIL AT SCHOOL.

WEAR THIS!

WE DIDN'T REALLY LIKE TO WEAR THE VEIL, ESPECIALLY SINCE WE DIDN'T UNDERSTAND WHY WE HAD TO.

IT'S TOO HOT OUT!

EXECUTION IN THE NAME OF FREEDOM.

GIVE ME MY VEIL BACK!

YOU'LL HAVE TO LICK MY FEET!

OOH! I'M THE MONSTER OF DARKNESS.

GIDDYAP!

AND ALSO BECAUSE THE YEAR BEFORE, IN 1979, WE WERE IN A FRENCH NON-RELIGIOUS SCHOOL.

WHERE BOYS AND GIRLS WERE TOGETHER.

AND THEN SUDDENLY IN 1980...

ALL BILINGUAL SCHOOLS MUST BE CLOSED DOWN.

THEY ARE SYMBOLS OF CAPITALISM.

BRAVO!

WHAT WISDOM!

OF DECADENCE.

THIS IS CALLED A "CULTURAL REVOLUTION."

WE FOUND OURSELVES VEILED AND SEPARATED FROM OUR FRIENDS.

AND THAT WAS THAT...

EVERYWHERE IN THE STREETS THERE WERE DEMONSTRATIONS FOR AND AGAINST THE VEIL.

AT ONE OF THE DEMONSTRATIONS, A GERMAN JOURNALIST TOOK A PHOTO OF MY MOTHER.

I WAS REALLY PROUD OF HER. HER PHOTO WAS PUBLISHED IN ALL THE EUROPEAN NEWSPAPERS.

AND EVEN IN ONE MAGAZINE IN IRAN. MY MOTHER WAS REALLY SCARED.

HAVE YOU SEEN THIS?

DON'T WORRY, DARLING.

SHE DYED HER HAIR,

AND WORE DARK GLASSES FOR A LONG TIME.

5

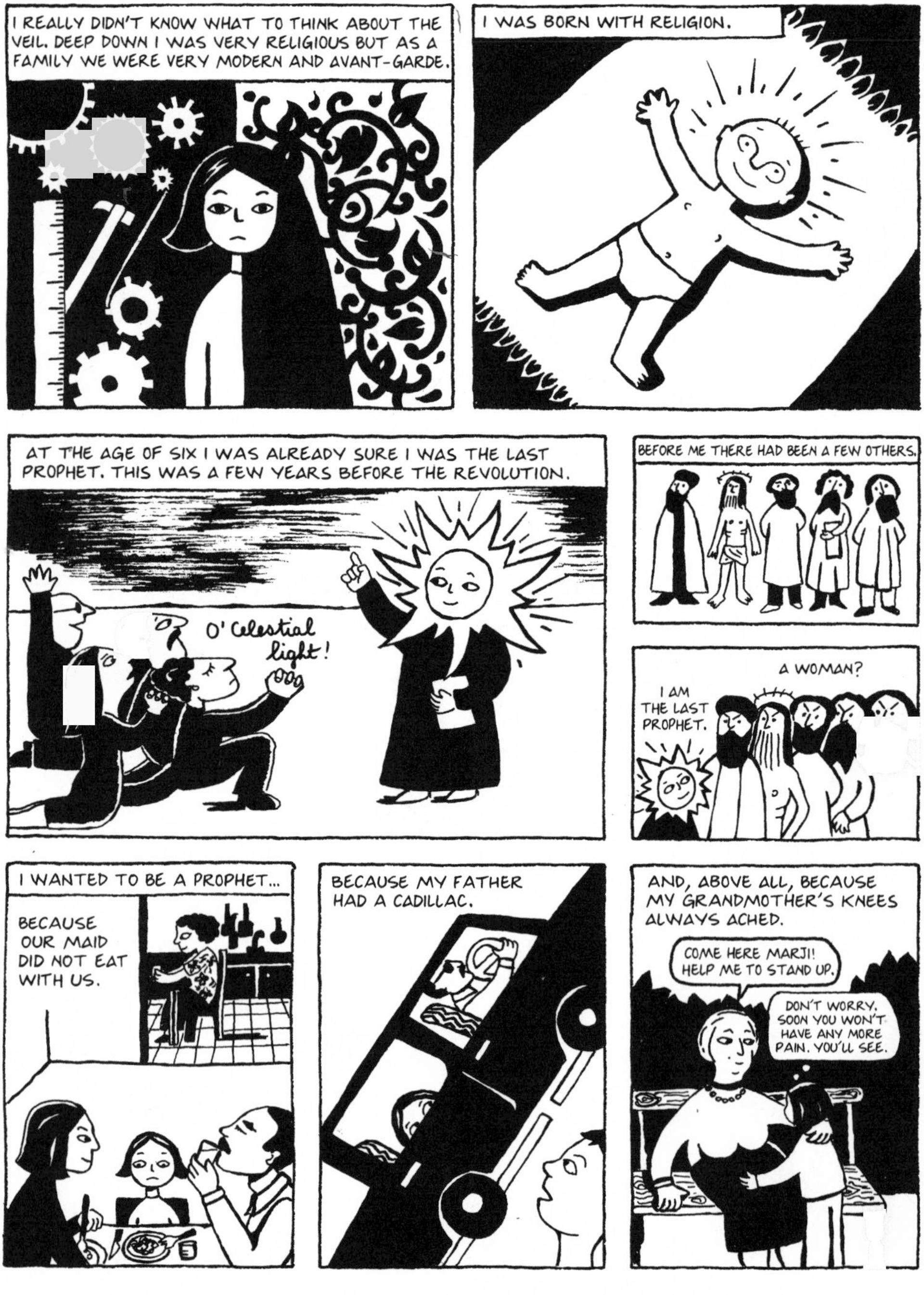
I REALLY DIDN'T KNOW WHAT TO THINK ABOUT THE VEIL. DEEP DOWN I WAS VERY RELIGIOUS BUT AS A FAMILY WE WERE VERY MODERN AND AVANT-GARDE.
I WAS BORN WITH RELIGION.
AT THE AGE OF SIX I WAS ALREADY SURE I WAS THE LAST PROPHET. THIS WAS A FEW YEARS BEFORE THE REVOLUTION.
O' Celestial light!
BEFORE ME THERE HAD BEEN A FEW OTHERS.
I AM THE LAST PROPHET.
A WOMAN?
I WANTED TO BE A PROPHET...
BECAUSE OUR MAID DID NOT EAT WITH US.
BECAUSE MY FATHER HAD A CADILLAC.
AND, ABOVE ALL, BECAUSE MY GRANDMOTHER'S KNEES ALWAYS ACHED.
COME HERE MARJI! HELP ME TO STAND UP.
DON'T WORRY. SOON YOU WON'T HAVE ANY MORE PAIN. YOU'LL SEE.

LIKE ALL MY PREDECESSORS I HAD MY HOLY BOOK.

THE FIRST THREE RULES CAME FROM ZARATHUSTRA. HE WAS THE FIRST PROPHET IN MY COUNTRY BEFORE THE ARAB INVASION.

YOU MUST BASE EVERYTHING ON THESE THREE RULES: BEHAVE WELL, SPEAK WELL, ACT WELL.

I ALSO WANTED US TO CELEBRATE THE TRADITIONAL ZARATHUSTRIAN HOLIDAYS. LIKE THE FIRE CEREMONY,

BEFORE THE PERSIAN NEW YEAR, NOROUZ, ON MARCH 21ST, THE FIRST DAY OF SPRING.

ONLY MY GRANDMOTHER KNEW ABOUT MY BOOK.

RULE NUMBER SIX: EVERY-BODY SHOULD HAVE A CAR.

RULE NUMBER SEVEN: ALL MAIDS SHOULD EAT AT THE TABLE WITH THE OTHERS.

RULE NUMBER EIGHT: NO OLD PER-SON SHOULD HAVE TO SUFFER.

IN THAT CASE, I'LL BE YOUR FIRST DISCIPLE.

REALLY?

BUT TELL ME HOW YOU'LL ARRANGE FOR OLD PEOPLE NOT TO SUFFER?

IT WILL SIMPLY BE FORBIDDEN.

EVERY NIGHT I HAD A BIG DISCUSSION WITH GOD.

GOD, GIVE ME SOME MORE TIME. I AM NOT QUITE READY YET.

YES YOU ARE, CELESTIAL LIGHT, YOU ARE MY CHOICE, MY LAST AND MY BEST CHOICE.

EXCEPT FOR MY GRANDMOTHER I WAS OBVIOUSLY THE ONLY ONE WHO BELIEVED IN MYSELF.

WHAT DO YOU WANT TO BE WHEN YOU GROW UP?

vion
A - a

I'LL BE A PROPHET.

HAHA! HAHA! HAHA!

SHE'S CRAZY.

MY PARENTS WERE CALLED IN BY THE TEACHER.

YOUR CHILD IS DISTURBED. SHE WANTS TO BECOME A PROPHET.

WHAT ABOUT IT?

DOESN'T THIS WORRY YOU?

NO! NOT AT ALL!

?

NONETHELESS, MY PARENTS WERE PUZZLED.

SO TELL ME, MY CHILD, WHAT DO YOU WANT TO BE WHEN YOU GROW UP?

A PROPHET.

I WANT TO BE A DOCTOR.

THAT'S FINE MY LOVE. THAT'S FINE.

I FELT GUILTY TOWARDS GOD.

YOU WANT TO BE A DOCTOR? I THOUGHT THAT...

NO, NO, I WILL BE A PROPHET BUT THEY MUSTN'T KNOW.

I WANTED TO BE JUSTICE, LOVE AND THE WRATH OF GOD ALL IN ONE.

THE BICYCLE

MY FAITH WAS NOT UNSHAKABLE.

THE YEAR OF THE REVOLUTION I HAD TO TAKE ACTION. SO I PUT MY PROPHETIC DESTINY ASIDE FOR A WHILE.

TODAY MY NAME IS CHE GUEVARA.

I AM FIDEL.

AND I WANT TO BE TROTSKY.

WE DEMONSTRATED IN THE GARDEN OF OUR HOUSE.

DOWN WITH THE KING!

DOWN WITH THE KING!

THE REVOLUTION IS LIKE A BICYCLE. WHEN THE WHEELS DON'T TURN, IT FALLS.

WELL SPOKEN!

AND SO WENT THE REVOLUTION IN MY COUNTRY.

"AFTER A LONG SLEEP OF 2500 YEARS, THE REVOLUTION HAS FINALLY AWAKENED THE PEOPLE."

"2500 YEARS OF TYRANNY AND SUBMISSION" AS MY FATHER SAID.

FIRST OUR OWN EMPERORS.

THEN THE ARAB INVASION FROM THE WEST.

FOLLOWED BY THE MONGOLIAN INVASION FROM THE EAST.

AND FINALLY MODERN IMPERIALISM.

TO ENLIGHTEN ME THEY BOUGHT BOOKS.

I KNEW EVERYTHING ABOUT THE CHILDREN OF PALESTINE.

ABOUT FIDEL CASTRO.

ABOUT THE YOUNG VIETNAMESE KILLED BY THE AMERICANS.

ABOUT THE REVOLUTIONARIES OF MY COUNTRY...

F. REZAÏ 1942-72

Dr. FATEMI 1928-58

H. ASHRAF 1938-72

BUT MY FAVORITE WAS A COMIC BOOK ENTITLED "DIALECTIC MATERIALISM."

IN MY BOOK YOU COULD SEE MARX AND DESCARTES.

THE MATERIAL WORLD DOESN'T EXIST, IT'S ONLY A REFLECTION OF OUR OWN IMAGINATION.

SAYS YOU!

YOU MEAN THAT EVEN THOUGH YOU SEE THIS STONE IN MY HAND IT DOESN'T EXIST SINCE IT'S ONLY IN YOUR IMAGINATION?

EXACTLY.

OUCH! WHAT ARE YOU DOING, KARL, YOU BROKE MY SKULL!

HA! HA! HA! HA! HA! HA! HA!

IT WAS FUNNY TO SEE HOW MUCH MARX AND GOD LOOKED LIKE EACH OTHER. THOUGH MARX'S HAIR WAS A BIT CURLIER.

DESPITE EVERYTHING, GOD CAME TO SEE ME FROM TIME TO TIME.

SO YOU DON'T WANT TO BE A PROPHET ANYMORE?

LET'S TALK ABOUT SOMETHING ELSE.

YOU THINK I LOOK LIKE MARX?

I TOLD YOU TO TALK ABOUT SOMETHING ELSE.

TOMORROW THE WEATHER IS GOING TO BE NICE.

?

IT WILL BE 75°F IN THE SHADE.

SHHH! WAIT A SECOND!

THEY BURNED DOWN THE REX CINEMA TONIGHT.

OH MY GOD.

THE DOORS HAD BEEN LOCKED FROM THE OUTSIDE A FEW MINUTES BEFORE THE FIRE.

THE POLICE WERE THERE.

THEY FORBADE PEOPLE TO RESCUE THOSE LOCKED INSIDE.

THEN THEY ATTACKED THEM.

14

THE FIREMEN DIDN'T ARRIVE UNTIL FORTY MINUTES LATER.

THE BBC SAID THERE WERE 400 VICTIMS. THE SHAH SAID THAT A GROUP OF RELIGIOUS FANATICS PERPETRATED THE MASSACRE. BUT THE PEOPLE KNEW THAT IT WAS THE SHAH'S FAULT!!!

EXIT

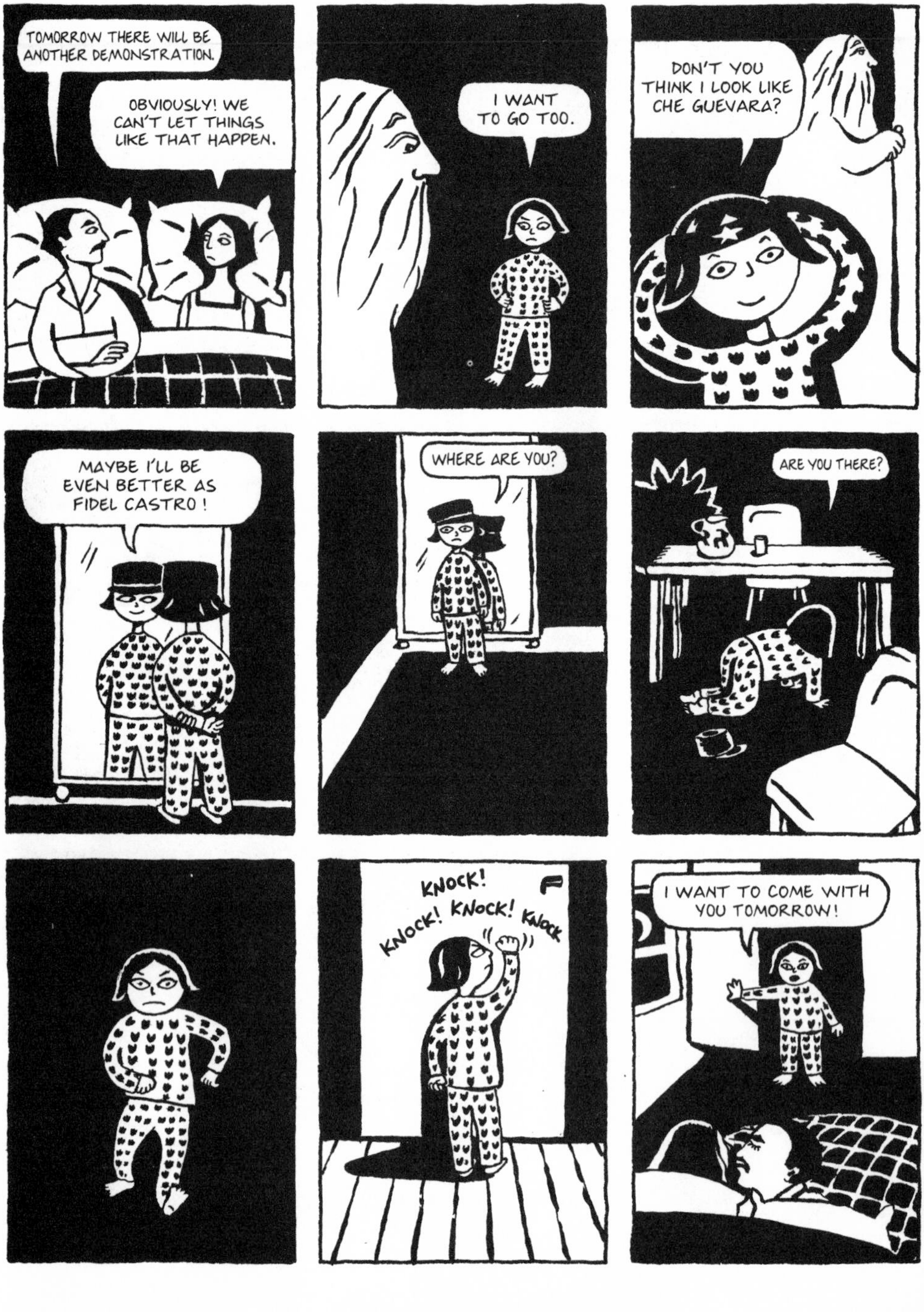
TOMORROW THERE WILL BE ANOTHER DEMONSTRATION.
OBVIOUSLY! WE CAN'T LET THINGS LIKE THAT HAPPEN.
I WANT TO GO TOO.
DON'T YOU THINK I LOOK LIKE CHE GUEVARA?
MAYBE I'LL BE EVEN BETTER AS FIDEL CASTRO!
WHERE ARE YOU?
ARE YOU THERE?
KNOCK! KNOCK! KNOCK! KNOCK
I WANT TO COME WITH YOU TOMORROW!

WHERE?

TO DEMONSTRATE ON THE STREET! I AM SICK AND TIRED OF DOING IT IN THE GARDEN.

IT IS VERY DANGEROUS. THEY SHOOT PEOPLE!

FOR A REVOLUTION TO SUCCEED, THE ENTIRE POPULATION MUST SUPPORT IT.

YOU CAN PARTICIPATE LATER ON.

SURE, SURE! WHEN IT'S ALL OVER.

MOM, PLEASE.

OH NO!

COME ON, YOU'RE GOING TO BED NOW.

PLEASE, PLEASE, PLEASE, PL...

GOD, WHERE ARE YOU?

THAT NIGHT HE DIDN'T COME.

THE WATER CELL

MY PARENTS DEMONSTRATED EVERY DAY.

DOWN WITH THE KING!

THINGS STARTED TO DEGENERATE. THE ARMY SHOT AT THEM.

AND THEY THREW STONES AT THE ARMY.

AFTER MARCHING AND THROWING STONES ALL DAY, BY EVENING THEY HAD ACHES ALL OVER, EVEN IN THEIR HEADS.

HEY MOM, DAD, LET'S PLAY MONOPOLY.

DARLING, WE ARE TIRED.

NOW IS NOT THE RIGHT TIME.

MONOPOLY! I CAN'T BELIEVE IT. HA! HA!

IT IS NEVER THE RIGHT TIME!

AS FOR ME, I LOVE THE KING, HE WAS CHOSEN BY GOD.

WHO TOLD YOU THAT?

MY TEACHER AND GOD HIMSELF.

COME SIT ON MY LAP. I'LL TRY TO EXPLAIN IT TO YOU.

GOOD, EXPLAIN EVERY-THING. I'M GOING TO BED.

GOD DID NOT CHOOSE THE KING.

HE DID SO! IT'S WRITTEN ON THE FIRST PAGE OF OUR SCHOOLBOOK.

THAT'S WHAT THEY SAY.

THE TRUTH IS THAT 50 YEARS AGO THE FATHER OF THE SHAH, WHO WAS A SOLDIER, ORGANIZED A PUTSCH TO OVERTHROW THE EMPEROR AND INSTALL A REPUBLIC.

IF IT IS GOD'S WILL, WE WILL REACH THE CAPITAL IN 19 DAYS.

GOD IS WITH US REZA, GOD IS WITH US.

AND EVEN IF HE ISN'T, WHAT CAN STOP US?

AT THE TIME THE REPUBLICAN IDEAL WAS POPULAR IN THE REGION BUT EVERYBODY INTERPRETED IT IN HIS OWN WAY.

GANDHI IN INDIA

THE HINDUS AND THE MUSLIMS MUST MAKE PEACE TO OVERTHROW THE BRITISH.

ATATURK IN TURKEY

WE, THE TURKS, ARE SECULAR WESTERNERS. FOR PROOF, LOOK AT MY GREEN EYES.

SO THE FATHER OF THE SHAH WANTED TO DO THE SAME,

BUT HE WASN'T EDUCATED LIKE GANDHI, WHO WAS A LAWYER...

...NOR WAS HE A LEADER OF MEN LIKE ATATURK, WHO WAS A GENERAL.

HE WAS AN ILLITERATE LOW-RANKING OFFICER.

A BLESSING FOR THE VERY INFLUENTIAL BRITISH WHO SOON LEARNED OF HIS PROJECTS.

THE COUNTRY IS RICH!

AND THE BOLSHEVIKS ARE NEAR.

WHAT'S THAT SOLDIER'S NAME AGAIN?

REZA! WE SHOULD GO MEET HIM.

IMMEDIATELY! PERSIA IS FULL OF OIL!

WELL REZA, SHI-NING YOUR BOOTS?

WHEN YOU ARE EMPEROR, YOUR SECRETARY OF STATE WILL SHINE THEM FOR YOU.

EMPEROR, ME?

BUT OF COURSE, MY FRIEND. IT'S MUCH BETTER THAN BEING PRESIDENT.

BUT THERE ALREADY IS AN EMPEROR! I WANT TO CREATE A REPUBLIC.

THE RELIGIOUS LEADERS ARE AGAINST IT AND THEY'RE RIGHT. A VAST COUNTRY LIKE YOURS NEEDS A HOLY SYMBOL.

YOU WILL HAVE EVERYTHING. POWER, SHOE SHINERS...

AND EVEN MORE. ANYTHING YOU WANT IN CASH!

WHAT DO I HAVE TO DO?

NOTHING!

YOU JUST GIVE US THE OIL AND WE'LL TAKE CARE OF THE REST.

AND THAT'S HOW HE BE-CAME KING AND NATURALLY HIS SON SUCCEEDED HIM. GOD HAS NOTHING WHATSOEVER TO DO WITH THIS STORY.

MAYBE GOD HELPED THEM NEVERTHELESS.

I THINK YOU ARE OLD ENOUGH TO UNDERSTAND CERTAIN THINGS. YOU SHOULD KNOW...

I SHOULD KNOW WHAT?

THE EMPEROR THAT WAS OVERTHROWN WAS GRANDPA'S FATHER.

MY GRAND-PA?

GRANDPA WAS A PRINCE?

YES, AMONG OTHERS. BUT THAT'S NOT THE QUESTION.

WHAT DO YOU MEAN, THAT'S NOT THE QUESTION?

My grandpa was a prince

AT THE TIME, YOUR GRANDPA WAS A YOUNG MAN AND THE FATHER OF THE SHAH CONFISCATED EVERYTHING HE OWNED.

DON'T FORGET THE TILES IN THE BATHROOM.

GO RIGHT AHEAD, DON'T LET ANYTHING STOP YOU.

AND SINCE HIS ENTOURAGE WAS UNEDUCATED, YOUR GRANDPA WAS NAMED PRIME MINISTER.

AS OF TODAY YOU ARE MY PRIME MINISTER.

YOU'RE PLEASED, AREN'T YOU? YOU HAVE DIPLOMAS, THEY HAVE TO BE PUT TO USE.

UHH...THANKS.

HE HAD STUDIED IN EUROPE. HE WAS A VERY CULTIVATED MAN. HE HAD EVEN READ MARX.

THE WORKERS! HOW CAN HE BELIEVE THAT THE RABBLE CAN RULE?

ONCE HE WAS SIDETRACKED FROM HIS PRINCELY DESTINY, HE BEGAN TO MEET INTELLECTUALS.

THE BOLSHEVIKS MAKE MIRACLES.

THE EMPEROR OF PERSIA IS NOT REZA SHAH BUT THE KING OF ENGLAND.

WHEN I WAS PRINCE, ALL OF THIS SEEMED SO DISTANT.

THAT IS REALLY THE PROBLEM OF OUR COUNTRY: ONLY A PRINCE CAN ALLOW HIMSELF TO HAVE A CONSCIENCE.

SO HE BECAME A COMMUNIST.

IT DISGUSTS ME THAT PEOPLE ARE CONDEMNED TO A BLEAK FUTURE BY THEIR SOCIAL CLASS. LONG LIVE LENIN.

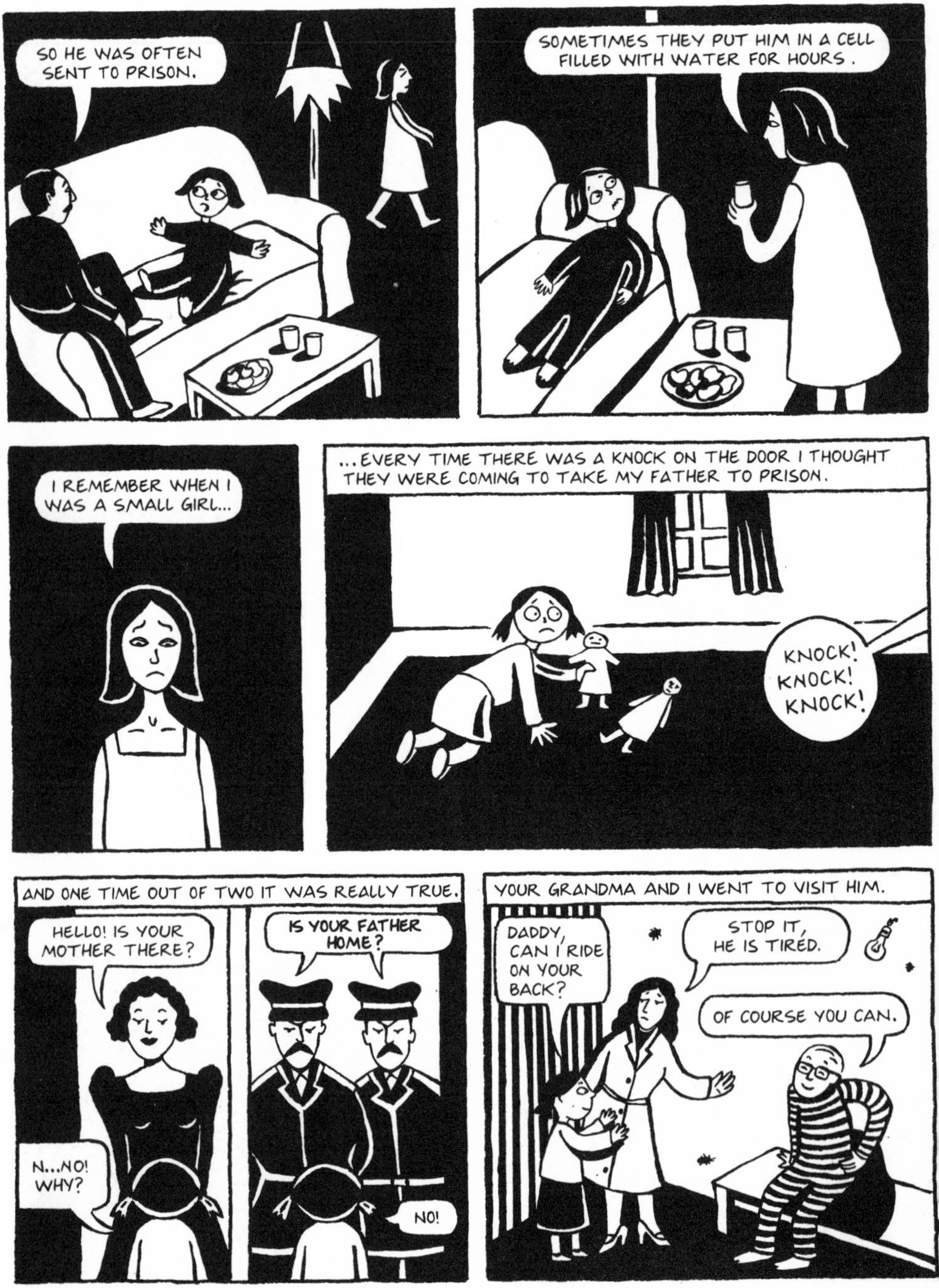
SO HE WAS OFTEN SENT TO PRISON.
SOMETIMES THEY PUT HIM IN A CELL FILLED WITH WATER FOR HOURS.
I REMEMBER WHEN I WAS A SMALL GIRL...
...EVERY TIME THERE WAS A KNOCK ON THE DOOR I THOUGHT THEY WERE COMING TO TAKE MY FATHER TO PRISON.
KNOCK! KNOCK! KNOCK!
AND ONE TIME OUT OF TWO IT WAS REALLY TRUE.
HELLO! IS YOUR MOTHER THERE?
N...NO! WHY?
IS YOUR FATHER HOME?
NO!
YOUR GRANDMA AND I WENT TO VISIT HIM.
DADDY, CAN I RIDE ON YOUR BACK?
STOP IT, HE IS TIRED.
OF COURSE YOU CAN.

GIDDYAP! GIDDYAP!

THE POOR MAN!!! PRISON HAD DESTROYED HIS HEALTH. HE HAD RHEUMATISM.

ALL HIS LIFE HE WAS IN PAIN.

COME ON. THAT TIME IS PAST.

DO YOU WANT TO PLAY MONOPOLY?

I WANT TO TAKE A BATH.

WE CAN PLAY AFTER YOUR BATH IF YOU WANT TO.

NO! I WANT TO TAKE A REALLY LONG BATH.

THAT NIGHT I STAYED A VERY LONG TIME IN THE BATH. I WANTED TO KNOW WHAT IT FELT LIKE TO BE IN A CELL FILLED WITH WATER.

WHAT ARE YOU DOING?

MY HANDS WERE WRINKLED WHEN I CAME OUT, LIKE GRANDPA'S.

 # PERSEPOLIS

ONE DAY AFTER SCHOOL...

HI, MOM.

HI. GO AND LOOK IN THE GUEST ROOM. THERE'S A SURPRISE FOR YOU.

GRANDMA!

ARE YOU LEAVING ALREADY?

NO, I'M JUST CHANGING.

MOM TOLD ME THAT GRANDPA HAD BEEN IN PRISON.

HMM, HOW WAS SCHOOL...

IT MUST HAVE BEEN VERY HARD ON YOU.

OH, MY BACK!

CAN I HELP YOU?

NO, I'M OK. AS YOU SAY, IT WAS VERY HARD FOR ME BUT ALSO FOR YOUR MOTHER AND FOR YOUR UNCLES.

THE SHAH'S FATHER TOOK EVERYTHING WE OWNED. I LIVED IN POVERTY.

WHAT? YOU MEAN YOU WERE POOR TOO?

OH, YES. SO POOR THAT WE HAD ONLY BREAD TO EAT. I WAS SO ASHAMED THAT I PRETENDED TO COOK SO THAT THE NEIGHBORS WOULDN'T NOTICE ANYTHING.

MMM! MOM IS COOKING SOMETHING GOOD!

COME ON! SHE IS JUST BOILING WATER AGAIN.

TO SURVIVE I TOOK IN SEWING AND WITH LEFTOVER MATERIAL, I MADE CLOTHES FOR THE WHOLE FAMILY.

LOOK HOW WELL DRESSED WE ALL ARE IN THIS PHOTO.

WHY ISN'T GRANDPA THERE? WAS HE IN PRISON?

YES, THE FATHER OF THE SHAH WAS VERY TOUGH BUT HIS SON WAS TEN TIMES WORSE.

EVEN WORSE!

YOU KNOW, MY CHILD, SINCE THE DAWN OF TIME, DYNASTIES HAVE SUCCEEDED EACH OTHER BUT THE KINGS ALWAYS KEPT THEIR PROMISES. THE SHAH KEPT NONE; I REMEMBER THE DAY HE WAS CROWNED. HE SAID:

I AM THE LIGHT OF THE ARYANS. I WILL MAKE THIS COUNTRY THE MOST MODERN OF ALL TIME. OUR PEOPLE WILL REGAIN **THEIR SPLENDOR.**

HE EVEN WENT TO THE GRAVE OF CYRUS THE GREAT, WHO RULED OVER THE ANCIENT WORLD.

CYRUS, REST IN PEACE, WE ARE LOOKING AFTER PERSIA.

ALL THE COUNTRY'S MONEY WENT INTO RIDICULOUS CELEBRA-
TIONS OF THE 2500 YEARS OF DYNASTY AND OTHER FRIVOLITIES...
ALL OF THIS TO IMPRESS HEADS OF STATE; THE POPULATION
COULDN'T HAVE CARED LESS.

I AM SO HAPPY THAT THERE IS
FINALLY A REVOLUTION BECAUSE
THE SHAH...

I'M HUNGRY!

I BOUGHT YOU SOME
BOOKS. YOU WILL SEE
WHY THE PEOPLE
ARE REVOLTING.

SHE WON'T
TELL ME ABOUT
GRANDPA.

YOUR DAUGHTER SAYS SHE IS HUNGRY!

WELL, SHE HAS TO WAIT FOR HER FATHER.

ʋшʍ#ҳʍ ʍʍ ʍʍ PHOTO!

ʌʊʍʍ ʊʍ !

HE'LL BE BACK SOON.

WHO?

MY FATHER HAD GONE TO TAKE SOME PHOTOS OF THE DEMONSTRATION BUT THIS TIME HE WAS VERY LATE.

HE TOOK PHOTOS EVERY DAY. IT WAS STRICTLY FORBIDDEN. HE HAD EVEN BEEN ARRESTED ONCE BUT ESCAPED AT THE LAST MINUTE.

WE WAITED FOR HIM FOR HOURS. THERE WAS THE SAME SILENCE AS BEFORE A STORM.

I THOUGHT THAT MY FATHER WAS DEAD, THAT THEY HAD SHOT HIM,

HELLO, I'M HOME!

EBY!

THANK GOD!

IF YOU ONLY KNEW HOW WORRIED I WAS!

SOMETHING INCREDIBLE HAPPENED!

YES, I ALMOST HAD A HEART ATTACK.

DAD!

I WAS SURE YOU WERE DEAD!

30

TODAY I WENT TO REY HOSPITAL WITH MY CAMERA.

PEOPLE CAME OUT CARRYING THE BODY OF A YOUNG MAN KILLED BY THE ARMY. HE WAS HONORED LIKE A MARTYR. A CROWD GATHERED TO TAKE HIM TO THE BAHESHTE ZAHRA CEMETERY.

THEN THERE WAS ANOTHER CADAVER, AN OLD MAN CARRIED OUT ON A STRETCHER. THOSE WHO DIDN'T FOLLOW THE FIRST ONE WENT OVER TO THE OLD MAN, SHOUTING REVOLUTIONARY SLOGANS AND CALLING HIM A HERO.

HERE IS ANOTHER MARTYR.

WELL, I WAS TAKING MY PHOTOS WHEN I NOTICED AN OLD WOMAN NEXT TO ME. I UNDERSTOOD THAT SHE WAS THE WIDOW OF THE VICTIM. I HAD SEEN HER LEAVE THE HOSPITAL WITH THE BODY.

PLEASE! STOP IT! STOP IT!

WHAT? WHAT IS IT?

STOP IT!

WHO ARE YOU?

HIS WIDOW!

ARE YOU A ROYALIST?

NO, BUT MY HUSBAND DIED OF CANCER...

31

WHAT?

OF WHAT?

WHAT IS SHE SAYING?

THE KING IS A KILLER! BUT HE WON'T BE A WINNER! WE WILL CATCH YOU ONE DAY! AND MAKE YOU PAY!

NO PROBLEM. HE'S A HERO.

BUT THE REST IS EVEN BETTER!

?

...BECAUSE THE WIDOW STARTED DEMONSTRATING WITH THEM.

THE KING IS A KILLER!

HA! HA!

IT'S TOO FUNNY!

IF I DIE NOW AT LEAST I WILL BE A MARTYR!!! GRANDMA MARTYR!

SOMETHING ESCAPED ME.

CADAVER, CANCER, DEATH, MURDERER

LAUGHTER?

HA! HA! HA! HA! HA! HA!

I REALIZED THEN THAT I DIDN'T UNDERSTAND ANYTHING. I READ ALL THE BOOKS I COULD.

THE REASONS FOR THE REVOLUTION

 # THE LETTER

I'D NEVER READ AS MUCH AS I DID DURING THAT PERIOD.

MY FAVORITE AUTHOR WAS ALI ASHRAF DARVISHIAN, A KIND OF LOCAL CHARLES DICKENS. I WENT TO HIS CLANDESTINE BOOK-SIGNING WITH MY MOTHER.

FER ME FRIEND KOUROSH.

WHY DOES HE SPEAK LIKE THAT?

IT'S JUST HIS KURDISH ACCENT.

HE TOLD SAD BUT TRUE STORIES: REZA BECAME A PORTER AT THE AGE OF TEN.

LEILA WOVE CARPETS AT AGE FIVE.

HASSAN, THREE YEARS OLD, CLEANED CAR WINDOWS.

GET DOWN FROM THERE, STUPID!

I FINALLY UNDERSTOOD WHY I FELT ASHAMED TO SIT IN MY FATHER'S CADILLAC.

THE REASON FOR MY SHAME AND FOR THE REVOLUTION IS THE SAME: THE DIFFERENCE BETWEEN SOCIAL CLASSES.

BUT NOW THAT I THINK OF IT... WE HAVE A MAID AT HOME!!!

HER

THIS IS MEHRI.

SHE WAS EIGHT YEARS OLD WHEN SHE HAD TO LEAVE HER PARENTS' HOME TO COME TO WORK FOR US. JUST LIKE REZA, LEILA AND HASSAN.

WE HAVE TOO MANY CHILDREN, 14 OR 15 INCLUDING HER.

SHE WILL EAT WELL AT YOUR HOUSE.

WE WILL TAKE CARE OF HER.

SHE WAS JUST TEN YEARS OLD WHEN I WAS BORN...SHE TOOK CARE OF ME.

SHE PLAYED WITH ME.

AND SHE ALWAYS FINISHED MY FOOD.

SHE ALSO TOLD ME STORIES ABOUT JACKALS THAT SCARED ME.

AND IT CAME CLOSER! AND IT CAME CLOSER!

IN OTHER WORDS, WE GOT ALONG WELL.

AT THE BEGINNING OF THE REVOLUTION, IN 1978, SHE FELL IN LOVE WITH THE NEIGHBOR'S SON. SHE WAS SIXTEEN YEARS OLD.

CAN YOU HELP ME LACE MY SHOES?

la la la la la la

EVERY NIGHT THEY LOOKED AT EACH OTHER FROM THE WINDOW OF MY ROOM.

UNTIL THE DAY HE SLIPPED HER A LETTER.

LIKE MOST PEASANTS, SHE DIDN'T KNOW HOW TO READ AND WRITE...

CAN YOU READ ME MY LETTER?

WHAT WILL YOU GIVE ME IN EXCHANGE?

MY MOTHER HAD TRIED TO TEACH HER BUT APPARENTLY SHE WAS NOT VERY TALENTED.

SO LET'S REPEAT. M AS IN...

CARROT!

SO I WROTE THE LETTERS FOR HER. ONE EACH WEEK FOR SIX MONTHS.

MY DEAR HOSSEIN, I MISS YOU A LOT. IT HAS BEEN THREE DAYS SINCE I SAW YOU AT THE WINDOW. I OFTEN TALK ABOUT YOU TO MY SISTER.

WHICH SISTER?

YOU!

I WAS VERY DEVOTED.

MEHRI HAD A REAL SISTER, ONE YEAR YOUNGER, WHO WORKED AT MY UNCLE'S HOUSE.

YOU KNOW, I HAVE A FIANCE.

OH REALLY, WHO?

IT'S HIM! IN FRONT OF THE TV. ISN'T HE HANDSOME?

NOT BAD!

AFTER A FEW VISITS, SHE FELL IN LOVE WITH HIM TOO.

HER JEALOUSY WAS MORE THAN SHE COULD BEAR AND SHE TOLD MEHRI'S STORY TO MY UNCLE, WHO TOLD IT TO MY GRANDMA, WHO TOLD IT TO MY MOM. THAT IS HOW THE STORY REACHED MY FATHER...

...WHO DECIDED TO CLARIFY THE SITUATION.

WHO'S THERE?

I AM YOUR NEIGHBOR. I WOULD LIKE TO HAVE A FEW WORDS WITH YOUR SON.

OK, I'LL GET STRAIGHT TO THE POINT: I KNOW THAT MEHRI PRETENDS SHE IS MY DAUGH- TER. IN REALITY SHE IS MY MAID.

REAL- LY?

BEE GEES

DO YOU WANT TO CONTINUE SEEING HER?

EHH...

BEE GEES

WITHOUT ANY HESITATION, HOSSEIN GAVE ALL THE LETTERS HE HAD RECEIVED TO MY FATHER!

BUT THIS IS MARJI'S HAND-WRITING!

TELL ME WHAT THESE ARE!

LETTERS!

WHY DIDN'T YOU TELL US ANYTHING?

YOU MUST UNDERSTAND THAT THEIR LOVE WAS IMPOSSIBLE.

WHY IS THAT?

BECAUSE IN THIS COUNTRY YOU MUST STAY WITHIN YOUR OWN SOCIAL CLASS.

BUT IS IT HER FAULT THAT SHE WAS BORN WHERE SHE WAS BORN???

DAD, ARE YOU FOR OR AGAINST SOCIAL CLASSES?

WHEN I WENT BACK TO HER ROOM SHE WAS CRYING. WE WERE NOT IN THE SAME SOCIAL CLASS BUT AT LEAST WE WERE IN THE SAME BED.

WHEN I FINALLY UNDERSTOOD THE REASONS FOR THE REVOLUTION I MADE MY DECISION.

TOMORROW WE ARE GOING TO DEMONSTRATE.

WE ARE NOT ALLOWED!

DON'T WORRY! WE ARE GOING ANYWAY!

SO THE NEXT DAY...

TAKE CARE!

MEHRI, DON'T FORGET TO COOK HER SOME CHICKEN.

YES, MADAM.

SEE YOU LATER!

FOR ONCE SHE DIDN'T INSIST ON COMING WITH US.

THERE IS THE DEMONSTRATION...

WE SHOUTED FROM MORNING TILL NIGHT.

38

IT'S LATE, WE HAVE TO GO HOME.

YES.

LONG LIVE THE REPUBLIC!

DOWN WITH THE SHAH!

GOOD LORD! WHERE THE DEVIL WERE YOU?

WE HAD DEMONSTRATED ON THE VERY DAY WE SHOULDN'T HAVE: ON "BLACK FRIDAY." THAT DAY THERE WERE SO MANY KILLED IN ONE OF THE NEIGHBORHOODS THAT A RUMOR SPREAD THAT ISRAELI SOLDIERS WERE RESPONSIBLE FOR THE SLAUGHTER.

BUT IN FACT IT WAS REALLY OUR OWN WHO HAD ATTACKED US.

✳ ✸ ✳ THE PARTY

AFTER BLACK FRIDAY, THERE WAS ONE MASSACRE AFTER ANOTHER. MANY PEOPLE WERE KILLED.

THE END OF THE SHAH'S REIGN WAS NEAR.

ONE DAY HE MADE A DECLARATION ON TV.

I UNDERSTAND YOUR REVOLT.

TOGETHER WE WILL TRY TO MARCH TOWARDS DEMOCRACY.

AFTER ALL THAT HE HAS DONE!

QUIET!

FOR A FEW MONTHS, HE ACTUALLY DID TRY: HE TESTED A DOZEN PRIME MINISTERS.

A FREEMASON? THAT'S NOT SUITABLE.

YOU REMIND THEM TOO MUCH OF MY FATHER!

TOO THIN!

TOO SHORT!

ONE-EYED!

....

THE MORE HE TRIED DEMOCRACY, THE MORE HIS STATUES WERE TORN DOWN.

PULL A LITTLE MORE TO THE LEFT.

...THEN HIS EFFIGY WAS BURNED.

THE PEOPLE WANTED ONLY ONE THING: HIS DEPARTURE! SO FINALLY...

OUT!

OUT!

OUT!

WE WILL NEVER FOR-GET YOU!

THE DAY HE LEFT, THE COUNTRY HAD THE BIGGEST CELEBRATION OF ITS ENTIRE HISTORY.

JIMMY CARTER, THE PRESIDENT OF THE UNITED STATES, REFUSED TO GIVE REFUGE TO THE EXILED SHAH AND HIS FAMILY.

IT LOOKS LIKE CARTER HAS FORGOTTEN HIS FRIENDS. ALL THAT INTERESTS HIM IS OIL!

IT'S ANWAR AL-SADAT WHO WILL ACCEPT HIM IN HIS COUNTRY.

WHO'S HE?

HE IS THE PRESIDENT OF EGYPT.

AND WHY IS HE TAKING IN THE SHAH?

THEY'VE BEEN FRIENDS FOR A LONG TIME. THEY BOTH BETRAYED THE COUNTRIES OF OUR REGION BY MAKING A PACT WITH ISRAEL.

IN ANY CASE, AS LONG AS THERE IS OIL IN THE MIDDLE EAST WE WILL NEVER HAVE PEACE.

LET'S TALK ABOUT SOMETHING ELSE. LET'S ENJOY OUR NEW FREEDOM!

NOW THAT THE DEVIL HAS LEFT!

MAYBE SADAT WELCOMED THE SHAH BECAUSE HIS FIRST WIFE WAS EGYPTIAN.

SURELY NOT! POLITICS AND SENTIMENT DON'T MIX.

AFTER ALL THIS JOY, A MAJOR MISFORTUNE TOOK PLACE: THE SCHOOLS, CLOSED DURING THIS PERIOD, REOPENED AND...

CHILDREN, TEAR OUT ALL THE PHOTOS OF THE SHAH FROM YOUR BOOKS.

BUT SHE WAS THE ONE WHO TOLD US THAT THE SHAH WAS CHOSEN BY GOD!

TEACHER! SHE SAYS THAT THE SHAH WAS CHOSEN BY GOD!!!

SATRAPI! YOU SHOULDN'T SAY THINGS LIKE THAT. STAND IN THE CORNER!

THESE STRANGE PHENOMENA WERE EVERYWHERE.

HELLO DEAR NEIGHBORS.

HELLO.

HELLO! ALL THOSE DEMON-STRATIONS WERE REALLY TIRING BUT WE FINALLY SUCCEEDED.

LOOK! A BULLET ALMOST HIT MY WIFE'S CHEEK. LIBERTY IS PRICELESS.

OH!

WHAT NERVE! SHE ALWAYS HAD THAT NASTY SPOT. IF WE WEREN'T NEIGHBORS, HE WOULD HAVE SAID SHE'S A MARTYR RAISED FROM THE DEAD.

IT IS NOT IMPORTANT.

THE BATTLE WAS OVER FOR OUR PARENTS BUT NOT FOR US.

MY FATHER SAYS RAMIN'S FATHER WAS IN THE SAVAK*. HE KILLED A MILLION PEOPLE.

A MILLION?

* SECRET POLICE OF THE SHAH'S REGIME.

IN THE NAME OF THE DEAD MILLION, WE'LL TEACH RAMIN A GOOD LESSON. I HAVE AN IDEA...

MY IDEA WAS TO PUT NAILS BETWEEN OUR FINGERS LIKE AMERICAN BRASS KNUCKLES AND TO ATTACK RAMIN.

RAMIN! RAMIN! COME OUT OF HIDING! DON'T BE A WIMP!

BUT MY MOTHER ARRIVED IN THE MIDDLE OF OUR EUPHORIA...

SO KIDS, WHAT ARE YOU UP TO?

MARJI FOUND SOME NAILS!!!

WE ARE GOING TO BEAT UP RAMIN!

HIS FATHER HAS KILLED A MILLION PEOPLE!

SO THAT'S WHAT YOU WANT, TO NAIL RAMIN? GET INTO THE CAR, I HAVE A BETTER SOLUTION.

REALLY? WHAT'S THAT?

WHERE DID YOU FIND THE NAILS?

IN DAD'S TOOL BOX!

WHAT WOULD YOU SAY IF I NAILED YOUR EARS TO THE WALL?

WOW! IT WOULD HURT A LOT.

I'LL LET IT GO THIS TIME. BUT DON'T DO IT AGAIN.

BUT MOM, RAMIN'S FATHER KILLED...

I KNOW.

HIS FATHER DID IT. BUT IT'S NOT RAMIN'S FAULT.

ANYWAY IT IS NOT FOR YOU AND ME TO DO JUSTICE. I'D EVEN SAY WE HAVE TO LEARN TO FORGIVE.

YOUR FATHER IS A MURDERER BUT IT'S NOT YOUR FAULT, SO I FORGIVE YOU.

HE IS NOT A MURDERER! HE KILLED COMMUNISTS AND COMMUNISTS ARE EVIL.

MOM, I SPOKE TO RAMIN. HE SAYS HIS FATHER DID THE RIGHT THING IN KILLING COMMUNISTS.

MY GOD! HE REPEATS WHAT THEY TELL HIM. HE WILL UNDERSTAND LATER...

YOU HAVE TO FORGIVE!

YOU HAVE TO FORGIVE!

I HAD THE FEELING OF BEING SOMEONE REALLY, REALLY GOOD.

THE HEROES

THE POLITICAL PRISONERS WERE LIBERATED A FEW DAYS LATER. THERE WERE 3000 OF THEM.

WE KNEW TWO OF THEM.

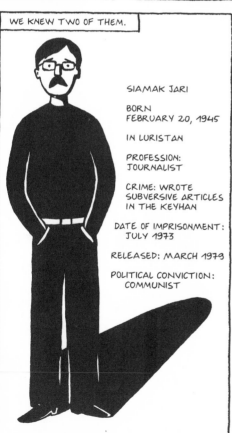

SIAMAK JARI

BORN
FEBRUARY 20, 1945

IN LURISTAN

PROFESSION:
JOURNALIST

CRIME: WROTE
SUBVERSIVE ARTICLES
IN THE KEYHAN

DATE OF IMPRISONMENT:
JULY 1973

RELEASED: MARCH 1979

POLITICAL CONVICTION:
COMMUNIST

MOHSEN SHAKIBA

BORN
NOVEMBER 22, 1947

IN RACHT

PROFESSION:
REVOLUTIONARY

CRIME:
REVOLUTIONARY

DATE OF IMPRISONMENT:
APRIL 1971

RELEASED: MARCH 1979

POLITICAL CONVICTION:
COMMUNIST

I HAD HEARD ABOUT SIAMAK EVEN BEFORE THE REVOLUTION. HE WAS THE HUSBAND OF MY MOTHER'S BEST FRIEND.

HOW LONG SINCE YOU HAD ANY NEWS ABOUT HIM?

TEN MONTHS??

BRING LALY WITH YOU AND COME BY TODAY. WE'LL TALK ABOUT IT.

LALY WAS SIAMAK'S DAUGHTER.

WHERE IS YOUR FATHER?

ON A TRIP.

DON'T YOU KNOW THAT WHEN THEY KEEP SAYING SOMEONE IS ON A TRIP IT REALLY MEANS HE IS DEAD?

AT LEAST THAT WAS THE CASE WITH MY GRANDPA.

BOO...HOO!

THE TRUTH IS SOMETIMES HARD TO ACCEPT.

BOO...HOO! MARJI SAYS... THAT DADDY... IS DEAD!

NO, NO... OF COURSE HE'S NOT.

GO TO YOUR ROOM AND STAY THERE!

NOBODY WILL ACCEPT THE TRUTH.

AFTER THE REVOLUTION I REALIZED THAT YOU COULD BE MISTAKEN.

TODAY IS A GREAT DAY, DARLING. WE'VE INVITED LALY'S FATHER AND MOHSEN. THEY BOTH JUST LEFT PRISON.

LALY'S FATHER?

WHAT DOES HE LOOK LIKE?

YOU'LL SOON FIND OUT.

DING! DONG!

SIAMAK!

I'M SO HAPPY THAT YOU ARE BACK...I DON'T KNOW WHAT TO SAY...

DON'T SAY ANYTHING. I KNOW!

OH TAJI! STILL A BEAUTY!

STILL A FLAT-TERER!

AND THIS MUST BE MARJI. LORD! THE LAST TIME I SAW HER SHE WAS ONLY THREE YEARS OLD.

TIME IS IRRETRIEVABLE. WHEN THEY ARRESTED ME, LALY BARELY SPOKE AND NOW SHE IS A REAL YOUNG LADY.

WELL, YES.

YES.

YOU WANT TO PLAY?

NO.

DING! DONG!

THAT MUST BE MOHSEN.

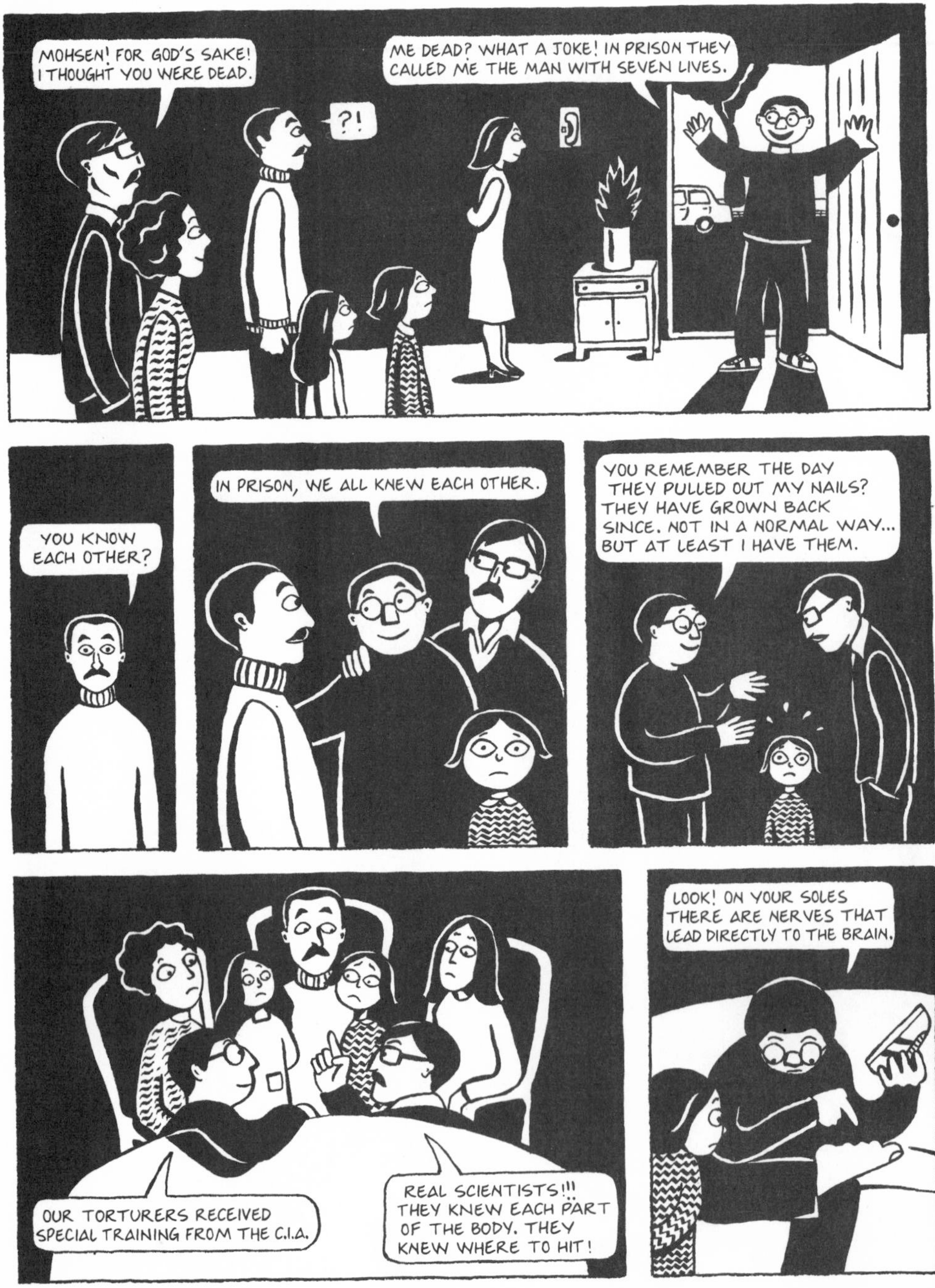
MOHSEN! FOR GOD'S SAKE! I THOUGHT YOU WERE DEAD.
?!
ME DEAD? WHAT A JOKE! IN PRISON THEY CALLED ME THE MAN WITH SEVEN LIVES.
YOU KNOW EACH OTHER?
IN PRISON, WE ALL KNEW EACH OTHER.
YOU REMEMBER THE DAY THEY PULLED OUT MY NAILS? THEY HAVE GROWN BACK SINCE. NOT IN A NORMAL WAY... BUT AT LEAST I HAVE THEM.
OUR TORTURERS RECEIVED SPECIAL TRAINING FROM THE C.I.A.
REAL SCIENTISTS!!! THEY KNEW EACH PART OF THE BODY. THEY KNEW WHERE TO HIT!
LOOK! ON YOUR SOLES THERE ARE NERVES THAT LEAD DIRECTLY TO THE BRAIN.

THEY WHIPPED ME WITH THICK ELECTRIC CABLES SO MUCH THAT THIS LOOKS LIKE ANYTHING BUT A FOOT.

NOT TO MENTION PUTTING OUT THEIR CIGARETTES ON OUR BACKS AND THIGHS...

MY PARENTS WERE SO SHOCKED...

THAT THEY FORGOT TO SPARE ME THIS EXPERIENCE...

ANY NEWS OF AHMADI?

AHMADI... AHMADI WAS ASSASSINATED. AS A MEMBER OF THE GUERILLAS, HE SUFFERED HELL. HE ALWAYS HAD CYANIDE ON HIM IN CASE HE WAS ARRESTED, BUT HE WAS TAKEN BY SURPRISE AND UNFORTUNATELY HE NEVER HAD A CHANCE TO USE IT... SO HE SUFFERED THE WORST TORTURE...

HOW DO YOU LIKE THIS?

CONFESS! WHERE ARE THE OTHERS!

THEY BURNED HIM WITH AN IRON.

I NEVER IMAGINED THAT YOU COULD USE THAT APPLIANCE FOR TORTURE.

IN THE END HE WAS CUT TO PIECES.

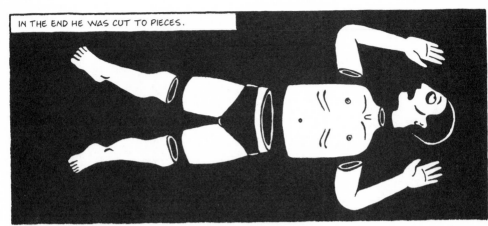

HE WAS IN MY CLASS AT THE UNIVERSITY.

IT'S A GOOD THING THEY DIDN'T KILL YOUR FATHER IN PRISON.

BUT YOU HAVE TO ADMIT I WASN'T COMPLETELY WRONG WHEN I SAID HE WAS NOT ON A TRIP.

MAYBE, BUT MY FATHER IS A HERO!

ALL TORTURERS SHOULD BE MASSACRED!

MY FATHER WAS NOT A HERO, MY MOTHER WANTED TO KILL PEOPLE...SO I WENT OUT TO PLAY IN THE STREET.

 THOSE STORIES HAD GIVEN ME NEW IDEAS FOR GAMES.

THE ONE WHO LOSES WILL BE TORTURED.

YEAH!

WHAT KIND OF TORTURE?

 I HAVE IMAGINA-TION TOO... THE MUSTACHE-ON-FIRE TORTURE CONSISTS OF PULLING ON THE TWO SIDES OF THE UPPER LIP.

 THE TWISTED ARM.

 THE MOUTH FILLED WITH GARBAGE.

 BACK AT HOME THAT EVENING, I HAD THE DIABOLICAL FEELING OF POWER...

 BUT IT DIDN'T LAST. I WAS OVERWHELMED.

 DON'T CRY DARLING. THEY WILL PAY FOR WHAT THEY HAVE DONE.

BUT I THOUGHT ONE SHOULD FORGIVE.

 BAD PEOPLE ARE DANGEROUS BUT FORGIVING THEM IS TOO. DON'T WORRY, THERE IS JUSTICE ON EARTH.

 I DIDN'T KNOW WHAT JUSTICE WAS. NOW THAT THE REVOLUTION WAS FINALLY OVER ONCE AND FOR ALL, I ABANDONED THE DIALECTIC MATERIALISM OF MY COMIC STRIPS. THE ONLY PLACE I FELT SAFE WAS IN THE ARMS OF MY FRIEND.

MOSCOW

SO MY FATHER WAS NOT A HERO.

IS EVERYTHING ALL RIGHT, MARJI?

YEAH, SURE...

IF ONLY HE HAD BEEN IN PRISON.

THEY CUT MY DAD'S LEG OFF, BUT HE STILL DIDN'T CONFESS!... SO THEY CUT OFF AN ARM AS WELL.

TOO MUCH!

LUCKILY, ONE DAY THEY TOLD ME ABOUT MY UNCLE ANOOSH.

THE ONLY ONE OF MY FATHER'S BROTHERS I HAD NEVER MET. BECAUSE HE HAD BEEN IN PRISON. AND NOW, FOR THE FIRST TIME IN 30 YEARS, MY GRANDMA WAS REUNITED WITH HER SIX CHILDREN.

AND I HAD A HERO IN MY FAMILY... NATURALLY I LOVED HIM IMMEDIATELY.

WHY DON'T YOU COME AND LIVE WITH US?

SUCH A SWEET CHILD! I'LL SLEEP HERE TONIGHT AND TELL YOU STORIES.

ARE YOU MARRIED? DO YOU HAVE CHILDREN? HOW OLD ARE YOU?

LATER MARJI, LATER.

DON'T BOTHER HIM TOO MUCH, HE'S TIRED.

GOOD NIGHT.

DON'T WORRY, WE'RE FINE.

OK, HERE GOES: I WAS 18 YEARS OLD WHEN MY UNCLE FEREYDOON AND HIS FRIENDS PROCLAIMED THE INDEPENDENCE OF THE IRANIAN PROVINCE OF AZERBAIJAN...

WOW!

FEREYDOON ELECTED HIMSELF MINISTER OF JUSTICE OF THIS NEW LITTLE REPUBLIC.

GENTLEMEN, JUSTICE IS THE BASIS OF DEMOCRACY. ALL MEN SHOULD BE EQUAL IN THE EYES OF THE LAW.

MY IDEAS WERE THE SAME AS HIS BUT YOUR GRANDFATHER REMAINED FAITHFUL TO THE SHAH.

MY SON, A TRAITOR! GO AWAY AND JOIN UP WITH MY IDIOTIC BROTHER!

YOU'LL BOTH END UP BEING EXECUTED! DO YOU HEAR ME? EXECUTED!

I BECAME FEREYDOON'S SECRETARY. IT WAS A TIME OF DREAMS AND ENTHUSIASM.

AZERBAIJAN IS ONLY THE BEGINNING. WE ARE GOING TO FREE IRAN PROVINCE BY PROVINCE!!!

I'M CERTAIN YOU'RE RIGHT, UNCLE.

ONE NIGHT I HAD A TERRIBLE NIGHTMARE: DEAD PEOPLE, BLOOD...

THE NEXT MORNING, I WAS SO TORMENTED. I HAD TO SEE FEREYDOON.

SHIT! THE SHAH'S SOLDIERS!

GOOD GOD! FEREYDOON!

I WANTED TO DO SOMETHING... BUT THERE WAS NOTHING I COULD DO...THEY ARRESTED HIM AND I RAN AWAY.

WHAT A STORY!

FOR DAYS AND DAYS I WALKED THROUGH THE FALLING SNOW. I CROSSED THE ALBORZ MOUNTAINS TO FIND REFUGE AT MY PARENTS' HOUSE IN ASTARA.

I WAS HUNGRY, I WAS COLD, BUT I CONTINUED.

I WAS NEARLY DEAD WHEN I ARRIVED.

BANG! BANG! BANG!

MY GOD! ANOOSH!!!

WHAT'S GOING ON? WHO'S BOTHERING US AT THIS HOUR?

COME QUICKLY! IT'S OUR SON ANOOSH! HE HAS FAINTED!

WHAT IS HE DOING HERE? WHY DIDN'T HE STAY WITH HIS NICE UNCLE?

YOU ALWAYS SAY THE RIGHT THING AT THE RIGHT TIME! HELP ME NOW!

OK, OK, CALM DOWN!

OH MY GOD... MY SON, MY DEAR SON...

IT'S A BIT LATE TO SHOW YOUR AFFECTION!!!

BUT THE SHAH'S POLICE WERE LOOKING FOR ME. I WAS NOT SAFE WITH MY PARENTS. SO I DECIDED TO GO INTO EXILE.

I SWAM ACROSS THE ARAS RIVER AND ARRIVED IN THE U.S.S.R.

HOLY SMOKE! LALY'S DAD HASN'T EVEN BEEN TO THE U.S.S.R.

WHAT HAPPENED TO YOUR UNCLE FEREYDOON?

HE MET HIS DESTINY...

I LEARNED THAT HE KNEW THE SHAH'S ARMY WAS COMING TO ARREST HIM. HE COULD HAVE RUN AWAY LIKE MOST OF HIS FRIENDS DID. BUT HE DECIDED TO STAY.

ALL IS LOST. I AM AT YOUR MERCY, GENTLEMEN.

AT THE TIME HE HAD A GIRLFRIEND WHO WAS INVOLVED IN HIS POLITICAL MOVEMENT. A GIRL FROM A GOOD FAMILY.

FEREYDOON, YOU HAVE A VISITOR.

MY LOVE...

MY DARLING, YOU SHOULDN'T HAVE COME, YOU ARE MAKING IT WORSE FOR YOURSELF.

LET'S MAKE A CHILD.

?

HERE? RIGHT NOW?

YES, I PAID THE GUARD. HE WON'T BOTHER US.

I AM GOING TO BE EXECUTED TOMORROW.

I KNOW, I WANT A LIVING MEMORY OF YOU.

YOU KNOW WHAT IT IS LIKE TO BE AN UNMARRIED MOTHER IN THIS COUNTRY. YOU WILL BE SHUNNED. LIFE WILL BE HELL.

I DON'T CARE. LET'S MAKE A CHILD.

SHE BECAME PREGNANT THAT VERY NIGHT AND LEFT FOR SWITZERLAND SOON AFTER. I KNOW THAT SHE HAD A SON. I HEARD HE LOOKS A LOT LIKE HIS FATHER.

ARE YOU ALRIGHT?

EHH...DO YOU HAVE OTHER STORIES LIKE THAT?

...? YES.

I'LL MAKE YOU A HOT CHOCOLATE.

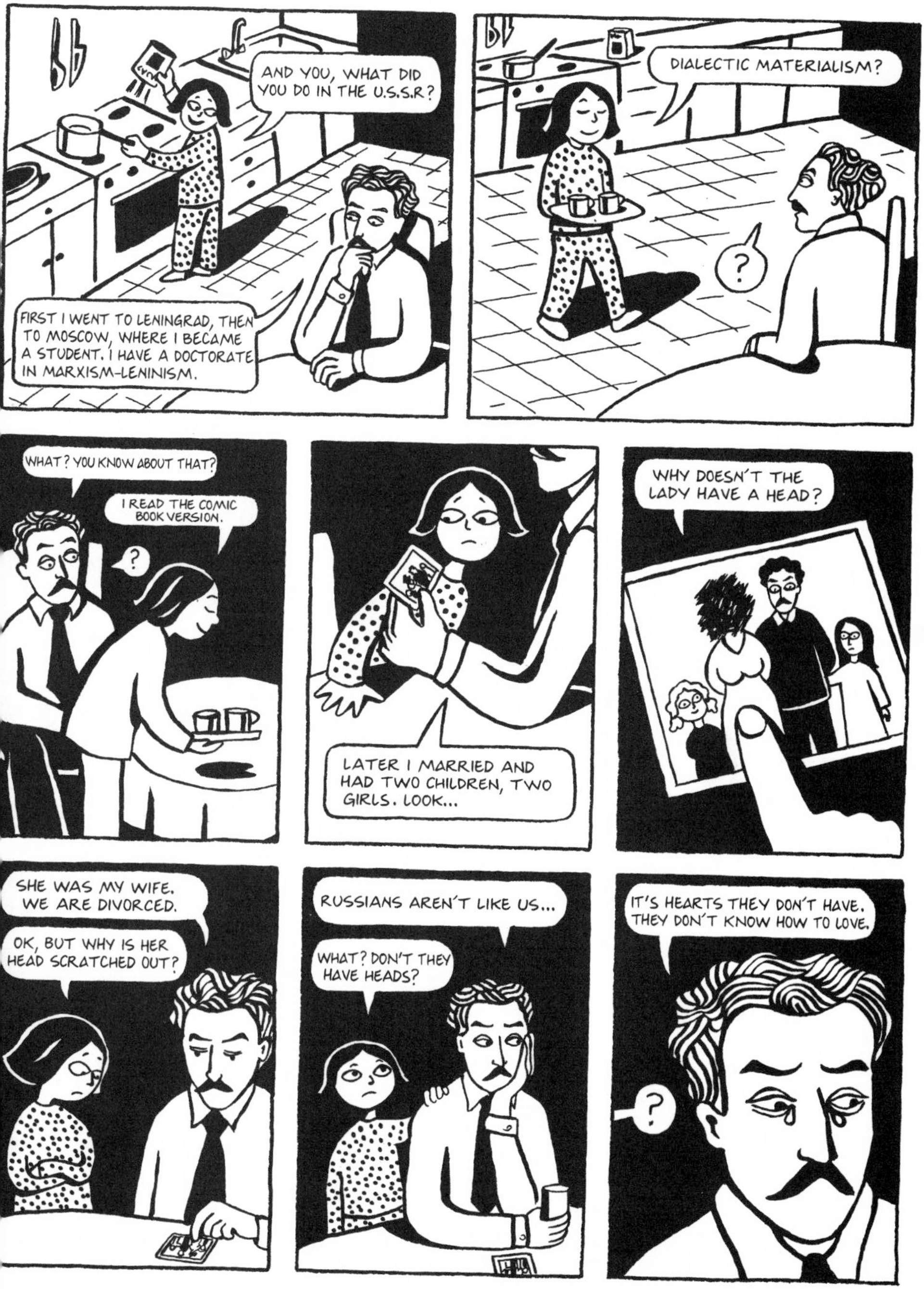
AND YOU, WHAT DID YOU DO IN THE U.S.S.R?
FIRST I WENT TO LENINGRAD, THEN TO MOSCOW, WHERE I BECAME A STUDENT. I HAVE A DOCTORATE IN MARXISM-LENINISM.
DIALECTIC MATERIALISM?
?
WHAT? YOU KNOW ABOUT THAT?
I READ THE COMIC BOOK VERSION.
?
LATER I MARRIED AND HAD TWO CHILDREN, TWO GIRLS. LOOK...
WHY DOESN'T THE LADY HAVE A HEAD?
SHE WAS MY WIFE. WE ARE DIVORCED.
OK, BUT WHY IS HER HEAD SCRATCHED OUT?
RUSSIANS AREN'T LIKE US...
WHAT? DON'T THEY HAVE HEADS?
IT'S HEARTS THEY DON'T HAVE. THEY DON'T KNOW HOW TO LOVE.
?

AFTER THE SEPARATION, I FELT VERY LONELY. I MISSED MY COUNTRY, MY PARENTS, MY BROTHERS. I DREAMT ABOUT THEM OFTEN.

I DECIDED TO GO HOME. I GOT A FALSE PASSPORT AND DISGUISED MYSELF.

I GUESS I WASN'T VERY CONVINCING. THEY SOON RECOGNIZED ME.

HEY! YOU WITH THE BEARD AND SUNGLASSES!

HALT!

THEY PUT ME IN PRISON FOR NINE YEARS.

NINE YEARS!

BETTER THAN LALY'S FATHER!

THEY SAY YOU WERE TORTURED TERRIBLY, LIKE SIAMAK, LALY'S FATHER.

YOUR FATHER TOLD YOU THAT?

NO, HE TOLD IT TO MOM AND I HEARD HIM.

WHAT MY WIFE MADE ME SUFFER WAS MUCH WORSE.

I TELL YOU ALL THIS BECAUSE IT'S IMPORTANT THAT YOU KNOW. OUR FAMILY MEMORY MUST NOT BE LOST. EVEN IF IT'S NOT EASY FOR YOU, EVEN IF YOU DON'T UNDERSTAND IT ALL.

DON'T WORRY, I'LL NEVER FORGET.

AND NOW IT'S TIME FOR BED!

WHAT? THE STORY'S FINISHED?

HERE, TAKE THIS SWAN I MADE IN PRISON. OUT OF BREAD.

IN PRISON?

PLEASANT DREAMS.

THERE ARE LOTS OF HEROES IN MY FAMILY. MY GRANDPA WAS IN PRISON, MY UNCLE ANOOSH TOO: FOR NINE YEARS! HE WAS EVEN IN THE U.S.S.R. MY GREAT-UNCLE FEREYDOON PROCLAIMED A DEMOCRATIC STATE AND HE WAS...

TOO MUCH!

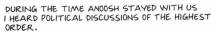 # THE SHEEP

DURING THE TIME ANOOSH STAYED WITH US I HEARD POLITICAL DISCUSSIONS OF THE HIGHEST ORDER.

IT'S INCREDIBLE. THE REVOLUTION IS A LEFTIST REVOLUTION AND THE REPUBLIC WANTS TO BE CALLED ISLAMIC.

IT'S NOT IMPORTANT. EVERYTHING WILL TURN OUT FINE. IN A COUNTRY WHERE HALF THE POPULATION IS ILLITERATE YOU CANNOT UNITE THE PEOPLE AROUND MARX. THE ONLY THING THAT CAN REALLY UNITE THEM IS NATIONALISM OR A RELIGIOUS ETHIC...

BUT THE RELIGIOUS LEADERS DON'T KNOW HOW TO GOVERN. THEY WILL RETURN TO THEIR MOSQUES. THE PROLETARIAT SHALL RULE! IT'S INEVITABLE!!! THAT'S JUST WHAT LENIN EXPLAINED IN "THE STATE AND THE REVOLUTION."

SOMETIMES I EVEN TOLD THEM MY OPINION...

ON TV THEY SAY THAT 99.99% OF THE POPULATION VOTED FOR THE ISLAMIC REPUBLIC.

DID YOU HEAR THAT, ANOOSH? DO YOU REALIZE HOW IGNORANT OUR PEOPLE ARE? THE ELECTIONS WERE FAKED AND THEY BELIEVE THE RESULTS: 99.99%!! AS FOR ME, I DON'T KNOW A SINGLE PERSON WHO VOTED FOR THE ISLAMIC REPUBLIC. WHERE DID THAT FIGURE COME FROM? FROM THEIR ASSES, THAT'S WHERE!

BUT IT'S NOT MY FAULT! IT'S THE TV!! BOO HOO!!!

CALM DOWN EBY, SHE'S JUST A CHILD WHO REPEATS WHAT SHE HEARS!

HEY, WANT TO PLAY?

HE'S GOING TO THE UNITED STATES!

TO THE UNITED STATES? WHY?

MY PARENTS SAY IT'S IMPOSSIBLE TO LIVE UNDER AN ISLAMIC REGIME, IT'S BETTER TO LEAVE.

BUT THE RELIGIOUS LEADERS ARE VERY STUPID, THEY WON'T LAST.

YEAH!

MY DAD SAYS NOBODY REALIZES THE DANGER.

SO WHEN ARE YOU LEAVING?

IN ABOUT A MONTH.

OH.

I THINK I REALLY LIKED THIS BOY...

BUT THE UNITED STATES IS TERRIFIC! YOU'LL FINALLY SEE BRUCE LEE IN PERSON!

YEAH...THAT WOULD BE NICE.

BRUCE LEE IS DEAD...

ACTUALLY I LIKED HIM VERY, VERY MUCH.

IT WAS THE END OF THE WORLD!...

AFTER MY FRIEND'S DEPARTURE, A GOOD PART OF MY FAMILY ALSO LEFT THE COUNTRY.

NOW BOARDING FLIGHT 6702 TO LOS ANGELES GATE 26. NOW BOARDING FLIGHT 6702 TO LOS ANGELES GATE 26.

MAYBE WE SHOULD LEAVE TOO...

SO THAT I CAN BECOME A TAXI DRIVER AND YOU A CLEANING LADY?

MY FRIEND KAVEH LEFT FOR THE UNITED STATES TOO.

DON'T WORRY. EVERYONE WHO LEFT WILL COME BACK. THEY'RE JUST AFRAID OF CHANGE.

LET'S HOPE SO!

I'M REALLY FRIGHTENED ANOOSH!

DON'T BE TAJI! IT'S LIKE THIS WITH ALL REVOLUTIONS. THIS IS JUST A TRANSITIONAL PERIOD...

RING! RING!

DAD! IT'S FOR YOU!!

WHAT?

WHAT'S GOING ON?

WHAT IS IT?

DAD!

YOUR MOTHER DIED?

IT'S MOHSEN,

HE'S BEEN FOUND DEAD, DROWNED...

...IN HIS BATHTUB.

WHAT?

WHERE?

MURDERERS! MURDERERS!

MY MOTHER WAS RIGHT TO BELIEVE IT WAS MURDER... WHEN THEY FOUND HIS BODY, ONLY HIS HEAD WAS UNDERWATER.

EVERYTHING WILL BE ALRIGHT!

AFTER MOHSEN, IT WAS SIAMAK'S TURN.

IS THIS SIAMAK JARI'S HOUSE?

YES!

WE ARE THE DELIVERERS OF DIVINE JUSTICE!

HIS SISTER WAS EXECUTED IN HIS PLACE.

DO YOU KNOW WHERE SIAMAK AND HIS FAMILY ARE NOW?

NO MORE THAN YOU DO, BUT THEY MUST SURELY HAVE HIDDEN SOMEWHERE.

AND LALY?

LATER ON WE LEARNED THEY CROSSED THE BORDER HIDDEN AMONG A FLOCK OF SHEEP.

EVERYTHING WILL BE ALRIGHT...

AND THAT IS HOW ALL THE FORMER REVOLUTIONARIES BECAME THE SWORN ENEMIES OF THE REPUBLIC.

WASN'T ANOOSH GOING TO PICK ME UP?

...

WHAT? WASN'T HE SUPPOSED TO COME?

WELL...

YES?

HE WENT BACK TO MOSCOW.

WHAT?

OH NO! THAT OLD TALE ABOUT BEING ON A TRIP HAD COME BACK...

HE HAD TO LEAVE QUICK-LY... HIS WIFE CALLED HIM. HE ASKED ME TO TELL YOU GOODBYE...

HE DOESN'T EVEN TALK TO HIS WIFE.

DARLING! DID YOU HAVE A GOOD DAY AT SCHOOL?

YOU MUST BE HUNGRY.

WHERE IS ANOOSH?

DON'T YOU WANT TO EAT A LITTLE?

I'M NOT HUNGRY.

WHY DIDN'T HE STAY TO SAY GOODBYE TO ME?

HE WAS IN A HURRY, A BIG HURRY.

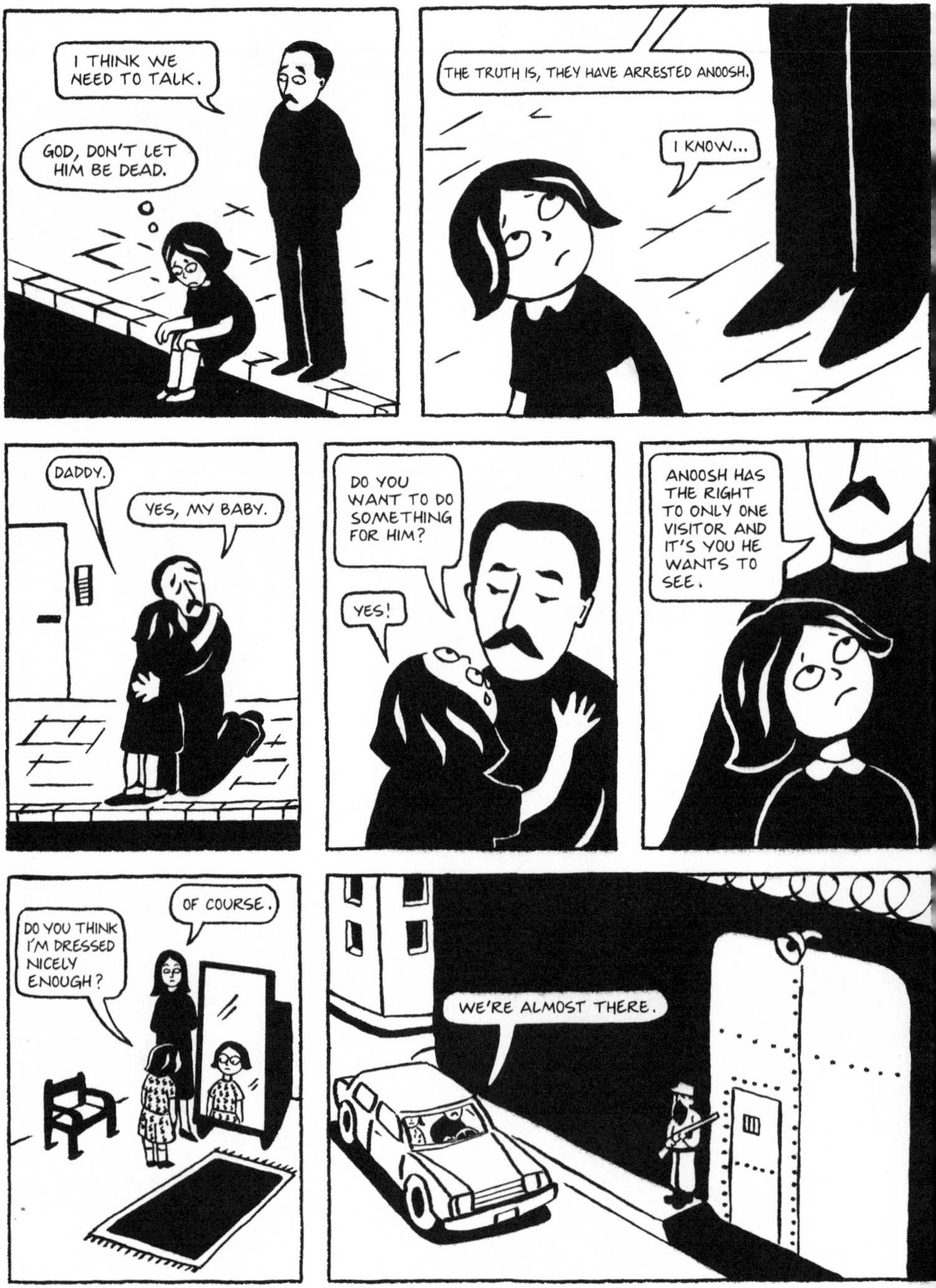
I THINK WE NEED TO TALK.
GOD, DON'T LET HIM BE DEAD.
THE TRUTH IS, THEY HAVE ARRESTED ANOOSH.
I KNOW...
DADDY.
YES, MY BABY.
DO YOU WANT TO DO SOMETHING FOR HIM?
YES!
ANOOSH HAS THE RIGHT TO ONLY ONE VISITOR AND IT'S YOU HE WANTS TO SEE.
DO YOU THINK I'M DRESSED NICELY ENOUGH?
OF COURSE.
WE'RE ALMOST THERE.

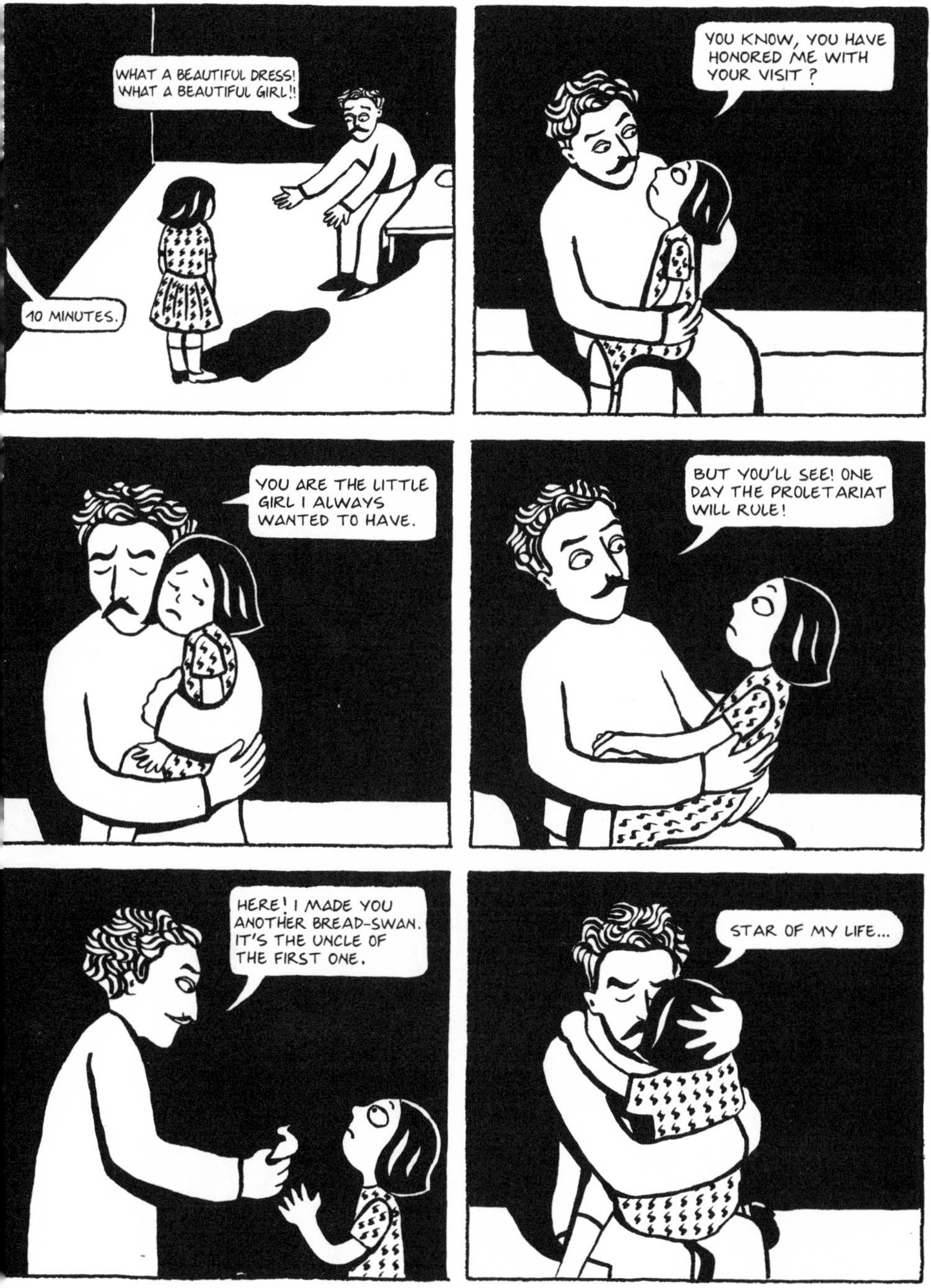
WHAT A BEAUTIFUL DRESS! WHAT A BEAUTIFUL GIRL!!
10 MINUTES.
YOU KNOW, YOU HAVE HONORED ME WITH YOUR VISIT ?
YOU ARE THE LITTLE GIRL I ALWAYS WANTED TO HAVE.
BUT YOU'LL SEE! ONE DAY THE PROLETARIAT WILL RULE!
HERE! I MADE YOU ANOTHER BREAD-SWAN. IT'S THE UNCLE OF THE FIRST ONE.
STAR OF MY LIFE...

THAT WAS MY LAST MEETING WITH MY BELOVED ANOOSH...

RUSSIAN SPY EXECUTED

see page 3

EVERYTHING WILL BE ALRIGHT...

MARJI, WHAT SEEMS TO BE THE PROBLEM?

SHUT UP, YOU! GET OUT OF MY LIFE!!! I NEVER WANT TO SEE YOU AGAIN!

GET OUT!

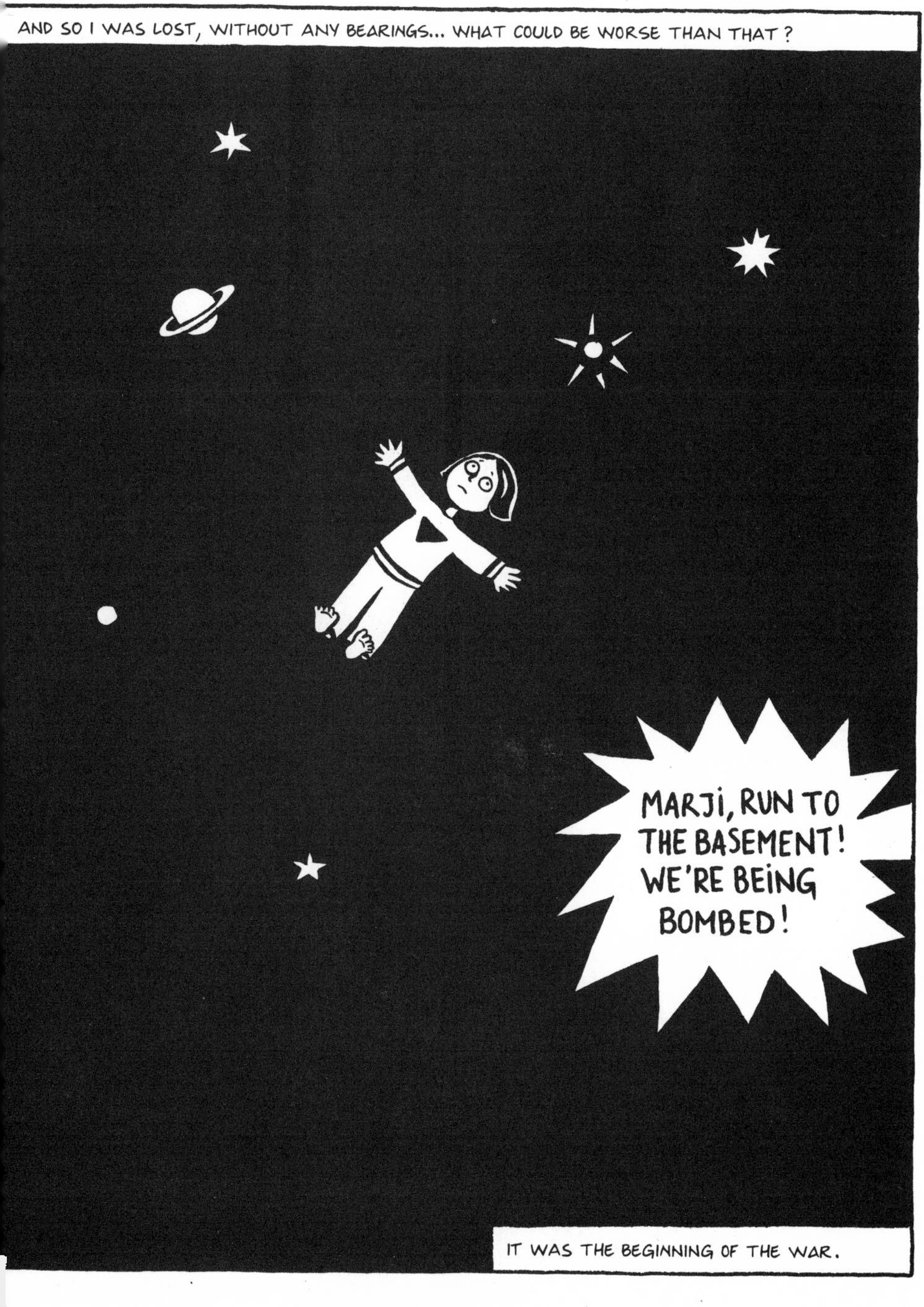
AND SO I WAS LOST, WITHOUT ANY BEARINGS... WHAT COULD BE WORSE THAN THAT?
MARJI, RUN TO THE BASEMENT! WE'RE BEING BOMBED!
IT WAS THE BEGINNING OF THE WAR.

THE TRIP

OH SHIT!

THEY'VE OCCUPIED THE U.S. EMBASSY!!

WHO'S "THEY"?

WHO DO YOU THINK? THE FUNDAMENTALIST STUDENTS HAVE TAKEN THE AMERICANS HOSTAGE!!

REALLY?

THEY CALL IT "A NEST OF SPIES." HA HA! YOU'D THINK IT WAS A JAMES BOND MOVIE.

YOU'RE NOT INTERESTED?

I COULDN'T CARE LESS.

ANYWAY, THE AMERICANS ARE DUMMIES.

MAYBE, BUT NOW NO ONE CAN GO TO THE UNITED STATES.

WHY'S THAT ??

THINK ABOUT IT. NO EMBASSY, NO VISA!

SO, MY GREAT DREAM WENT UP IN SMOKE. I WOULDN'T BE ABLE TO GO TO THE UNITED STATES.

KAVEH, THEY CLOSED THE U.S. EMBASSY TODAY. I WON'T BE ABLE TO COME AND SEE YOU...

THE DREAM WASN'T THE USA. IT WAS SEEING MY FRIEND KAVEH WHO HAD LEFT TO GO LIVE IN THE STATES A YEAR EARLIER.

AND THEN SOME DAYS LATER...

THE MINISTERY OF EDUCATION HAS DECREED THAT UNIVERSITIES WILL CLOSE AT THE END OF THE MONTH.

OH NO!

THE EDUCATIONAL SYSTEM AND WHAT IS WRITTEN IN SCHOOL BOOKS, AT ALL LEVELS, ARE DECADENT. EVERYTHING NEEDS TO BE REVISED TO ENSURE THAT OUR CHILDREN ARE NOT LED ASTRAY FROM THE TRUE PATH OF ISLAM.

OF COURSE, OF COURSE!

THAT'S WHY WE'RE CLOSING ALL THE UNIVERSITIES FOR A WHILE. BETTER TO HAVE NO STUDENTS AT ALL THAN TO EDUCATE FUTURE IMPERIALISTS.

THUS, THE UNIVERSITIES WERE CLOSED FOR TWO YEARS.

YOU'LL SEE. SOON THEY'RE ACTUALLY GOING TO FORCE US TO WEAR THE VEIL AND YOU, YOU'LL HAVE TO TRADE YOUR CAR FOR A CAMEL. GOD, WHAT A BACKWARD POLICY!

A CAMEL?

NO MORE UNIVERSITY. AND I WANTED TO STUDY CHEMISTRY. I WANTED TO BE LIKE MARIE CURIE.

I WANTED TO BE AN EDUCATED, LIBERATED WOMAN. AND IF THE PURSUIT OF KNOWLEDGE MEANT GETTING CANCER, SO BE IT.

IT'S I WHO DISCOVERED THE NEWEST RADIOACTIVE ELEMENT.

AND SO ANOTHER DREAM WENT UP IN SMOKE.

MISERY! AT THE AGE THAT MARIE CURIE FIRST WENT TO FRANCE TO STUDY, I'LL PROBABLY HAVE TEN CHILDREN ...

ONE NIGHT...

YOUR MOTHER'S CAR BROKE DOWN, WE HAVE TO PICK HER UP.

EBi!

MOM!

TWO GUYS...TWO BEARDED GUYS!... TWO FUNDAMENTALIST BASTARDS... THE BASTARDS...THE BASTARDS...THEY...

CALM DOWN DARLING, CALM DOWN, WHAT DID THEY DO?

MOM!

THEY INSULTED ME. THEY SAID THAT WOMEN LIKE ME SHOULD BE PUSHED UP AGAINST A WALL AND FUCKED, AND THEN THROWN IN THE GARBAGE.

...AND THAT IF I DIDN'T WANT THAT TO HAPPEN, I SHOULD WEAR THE VEIL...

FORGET ABOUT THOSE MORONS!! LET'S GO HOME...

THAT INCIDENT MADE MY MOTHER SICK FOR SEVERAL DAYS.

ANYTHING I CAN GET YOU, MOM?

...

AND SO TO PROTECT WOMEN FROM ALL THE POTENTIAL RAPISTS, THEY DECREED THAT WEARING THE VEIL WAS OBLIGATORY.

WOMEN'S HAIR EMANATES RAYS THAT EXCITE MEN. THAT'S WHY WOMEN SHOULD COVER THEIR HAIR! IF IN FACT IT IS REALLY MORE CIVILIZED TO GO WITHOUT THE VEIL, THEN ANIMALS ARE MORE CIVILIZED THAN WE ARE.

INCREDIBLE! THEY THINK ALL MEN ARE PERVERTS!!

OF COURSE, BECAUSE THEY REALLY ARE PERVERTS!

IN NO TIME, THE WAY PEOPLE DRESSED BECAME AN IDEOLOGICAL SIGN. THERE WERE TWO KINDS OF WOMEN.

THE FUNDAMENTALIST WOMAN

THE MODERN WOMAN

YOU SHOWED YOUR OPPOSITION TO THE REGIME BY LETTING A FEW STRANDS OF HAIR SHOW.

THERE WERE ALSO TWO SORTS OF MEN.

THE FUNDAMENTALIST MAN

BEARD   SHIRT HANGING OUT

THE PROGRESSIVE MAN

SHAVED, WITH OR WITHOUT MUSTACHE   SHIRT TUCKED IN

ISLAM IS MORE OR LESS AGAINST SHAVING.

BUT LET'S BE FAIR. IF WOMEN FACED PRISON WHEN THEY REFUSED TO WEAR THE VEIL, IT WAS ALSO FORBIDDEN FOR MEN TO WEAR NECKTIES (THAT DREADED SYMBOL OF THE WEST). AND IF WOMEN'S HAIR GOT MEN EXCITED, THE SAME THING COULD BE SAID OF MEN'S BARE ARMS. AND SO, WEARING SHORT-SLEEVED SHIRTS WAS ALSO FORBIDDEN.

THERE WAS A KIND OF JUSTICE, AFTER ALL.

IT WASN'T ONLY THE GOVERNMENT THAT CHANGED. ORDINARY PEOPLE CHANGED TOO.

LOOK AT HER! LAST YEAR SHE WAS WEARING A MINISKIRT, SHOWING OFF HER BEEFY THIGHS TO THE WHOLE NEIGHBORHOOD. AND NOW MADAME IS WEARING A CHADOR. IT SUITS HER BETTER, I GUESS.

S FOR HER FUNDAMENTALIST HUSBAND WHO RANK HIMSELF INTO A STUPOR EVERY IGHT, NOW HE USES MOUTHWASH EVERY TIME HE UTTERS THE WORD "ALCOHOL."

AND THEIR SON SAYS HE PRAYS EVERY DAY!

IF ANYONE EVER ASKS YOU WHAT YOU DO DURING THE DAY, SAY YOU PRAY, YOU UNDERSTAND??

OK...

AT FIRST, IT WAS A LITTLE HARD, BUT I LEARNED TO LIE QUICKLY.

I PRAY FIVE TIMES A DAY.

ME? TEN OR ELEVEN TIMES... SOMETIMES TWELVE.

IN SPITE OF EVERYTHING, THE SPIRIT OF REVOLUTION WAS STILL IN THE AIR. THERE WERE SOME OPPOSITION DEMONSTRATIONS.

TOMORROW THERE'S GOING TO BE A MEETING AGAINST FUNDAMENTALISM.

I'M COMING TOO!

NO! IT'S TOO DANGEROUS.

SHE'S COMING TOO.

SHE SHOULD START LEARNING TO DEFEND HER RIGHTS AS A WOMAN RIGHT NOW!

SINCE THE 1979 REVOLUTION, I'D GROWN OLDER (WELL, A YEAR OLDER) AND MOM HAD CHANGED.

SO I WENT WITH THEM. I PASSED OUT FLYERS...

GUNS MAY SHOOT AND KNIVES MAY CARVE, BUT WE WON'T WEAR YOUR SILLY SCARVES!

...WHEN SUDDENLY THINGS GOT NASTY.

THE SCARF OR A BEATING!

FOR THE FIRST TIME IN MY LIFE, I SAW VIOLENCE WITH MY OWN EYES.

DAD!

THAT WAS OUR LAST DEMONSTRATION.

EVERY MAN FOR HIMSELF!

THINGS GOT WORSE FROM ONE DAY TO THE NEXT. IN SEPTEMBER 1980, MY PARENTS ABRUPTLY PLANNED A VACATION. I THINK THEY REALIZED THAT SOON SUCH THINGS WOULD NO LONGER BE POSSIBLE. AS IT HAPPENED, THEY WERE RIGHT. AND SO WE WENT TO ITALY AND SPAIN FOR THREE WEEKS...

...IT WAS WONDERFUL.

RIGHT BEFORE GOING BACK, IN THE HOTEL ROOM IN MADRID.

LOOK AT THIS.

THE TV SHOWED A MAP OF IRAN AND A BLACK CLOUD COVERING THE COUNTRY LITTLE BY LITTLE.

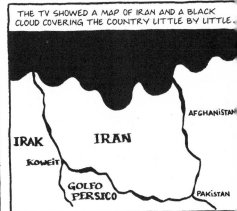

WHAT IN THE WORLD IS THIS?

TOO BAD WE DON'T KNOW SPANISH.

MAYBE THEY'RE TALKING ABOUT POLLUTION. YOU KNOW, TEHRAN IS THE FOURTH MOST POLLUTED CITY IN THE WORLD.

IT LOOKS LIKE THEY'RE TALKING ABOUT THE WHOLE COUNTRY, NOT JUST THE CAPITAL.

THE NEXT DAY MY GRANDMOTHER CAME TO PICK US UP AT THE AIRPORT.

GRANDMA! I GOT YOU A BLACK DRESS!

SHE LOOKED WORRIED.

EVERYTHING OK, MOM?

YES...

OH! I'M TAKING THIS THING OFF. IT'S TOO HOT.

IT'S GOOD TO BE BACK. THERE'S NO PLACE LIKE HOME.

TRUE. BUT SOON THERE'LL BE NO HOME.

WHY DO YOU SAY THAT?

YOU HAVEN'T HEARD?

HAVEN'T HEARD WHAT?

WE'RE AT WAR!

WHAT!?

...THEY ONLY OFFICIALLY ANNOUNCED IT TWO DAYS AGO, BUT REALLY, IT'S BEEN A MONTH... THE IRANIAN FUNDAMENTALISTS TRIED TO STIR UP THEIR IRAQI SHIITE ALLIES AGAINST SADDAM. HE'S BEEN WAITING FOR THE CHANCE. HE'S ALWAYS WANTED TO INVADE IRAN. AND HERE'S THE PRETEXT. IT'S THE SECOND ARAB INVASION...

THE SECOND INVASION IN 1400 YEARS! MY BLOOD WAS BOILING. I WAS READY TO DEFEND MY COUNTRY AGAINST THESE ARABS WHO KEPT ATTACKING US.

I WANTED TO FIGHT.

THE F-14s

A FEW DAYS AFTER OUR TRIP, AND JUST BEFORE I HAD TO GO BACK TO SCHOOL, I WENT TO MY FATHER'S OFFICE.

TYPE THIS AND MAKE THREE COPIES.

OK

BOOM

HELP!!

IT WAS THE FIRST TIME I'D SEEN FIGHTER JETS...

TOO MUCH! IT'S OUR ARMY FLYING!

I DON'T THINK SO. THOSE ARE PROBABLY IRAQIS.

WHAT? WHY DO YOU SAY THAT???

BECAUSE THEY DON'T LOOK LIKE OUR F-14S!

IT WAS A TOUGH CALL, BUT DAD WAS AN ENGINEER. HE WAS THE SPECIALIST.

IRANIAN OR IRAQI, THE JETS HUGGED THE GROUND BEFORE SUDDENLY ZOOMING UP INTO THE SKY RIGHT BEFORE THE MOUNTAINS ON THE HORIZON.

QUICK, THE RADIO.

HERE, DAD!

IRAQI MIGS HAVE BOMBED TEHRAN...

NO! THE BASTARDS!

THOSE ASSHOLES!

LET'S GO HOME NOW! YOUR MOTHER MUST BE TERRIFIED.

DAD! DO YOU REMEMBER WHAT YOU LEARNED DURING YOUR MILITARY SERVICE? ARE YOU GOING TO WAR? ARE YOU GOING TO FIGHT? WE HAVE TO TEACH THOSE IRAQIS A LESSON!

WHAT ARE YOU TALKING ABOUT? OF COURSE I'M NOT GOING TO FIGHT. WHY SHOULD I FIGHT?!

HOW CAN YOU SAY THAT? THE IRAQIS HAVE ALWAYS BEEN OUR ENEMIES. THEY WANT TO INVADE US.

AND WORSE, THEY DRIVE LIKE MANIACS...

THE ARABS NEVER LIKED THE PERSIANS. EVERYONE KNOWS THAT. THEY ATTACKED US 1400 YEARS AGO. THEY FORCED THEIR RELIGION ON US.

OK, ENOUGH OF THAT. THE REAL ISLAMIC INVASION HAS COME FROM OUR OWN GOVERNMENT.

TAJI!

MOM!

TAJI!?

DARLING

?

MOM

THE IRAQIS BOMBED US!

REALLY? WHEN?

JUST NOW!

WELL, I GUESS I SHOULD DRY OFF.

WAR ALWAYS TAKES YOU BY SURPRISE.

WE HAVE TO BOMB BAGHDAD!

TAKE YOUR FEET OFF THE TABLE, IT'S IMPOLITE.

BOMB BAGHDAD...YOU NEED PILOTS FOR THAT. AFTER THE GENERALS BLEW THEIR CHANCE AT A COUP D'ETAT, THEY WERE ALL JAILED OR EXECUTED...

WHAT'S THIS ABOUT? COUP D'ETAT? PILOTS IN JAIL? WHAT PILOTS?

I KNEW FIGHTER PILOTS. MY FRIEND PARDISSE'S FATHER WAS ONE.

SHE NEVER TOLD ME HER FATHER WAS IN PRISON! ALTHOUGH LAST YEAR SHE DIDN'T COME TO SCHOOL FOR A WHOLE MONTH.

THAT BASTARD SADDAM WAITED UNTIL WE WERE WEAK BEFORE ATTACKING!

PARDISSE ENTEZAMI'S DAD IS A FIGHTER PILOT. HE'S GOING TO GO BOMB BAGHDAD.

ENTEZAMI...ENTEZAMI... HE WAS ONE OF THE CONDEMNED. FIRST HE HAS TO GET OUT OF PRISON!

I'M GOING TO MY ROOM.

IT'S THE PITS! MY DAD IS A DEFEATIST. HE'S NO PATRIOT...

SUDDENLY, I HEARD THE IRANIAN NATIONAL ANTHEM COMING FROM THE TV. OUR STAR-SPANGLED BANNER.

♫ OH IRAN, OUR GOLDEN ♫ COUNTRY, YOUR LAND IS THE WELLSPRING OF ART ♫♫

IT HAD BEEN FORBIDDEN AND REPLACED BY THE NEW GOVERNMENT'S ISLAMIC HYMN...

IT HAD BEEN MORE THAN A YEAR SINCE WE'D HEARD IT...

♫ LET THE EVIL THOUGHTS OF YOUR ENEMIES BE FAR FROM YOU ♫♫

WE WERE OVERWHELMED...

WELCOME TO THE 8:00 NEWS. 140 IRANIAN F-14S CARRIED OUT BOMBING RAIDS ON BAGHDAD TONIGHT.

WELL, THERE'S YOUR PROOF THAT OUR ARMY IS STILL STRONG!

YOU CAN'T ALWAYS BELIEVE WHAT THEY SAY. 8 O'CLOCK. THE BBC IS BROADCASTING TOO. WHERE'S THE RADIO?

YOU DON'T BELIEVE ANYTHING! HERE'S THE RADIO!

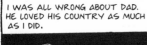

I WAS ALL WRONG ABOUT DAD. HE LOVED HIS COUNTRY AS MUCH AS I DID.

...THE REST OF THE NEWS WASN'T SO COOL...

IRANIAN LOSSES WERE VERY HEAVY... HALF OF THE PLANES IN THE MISSION HAVE NOT RETURNED.

I HOPE PARDISSE'S DAD ISN'T DEAD!

CALL HER.

I DON'T HAVE HER NUMBER.

I HAD TO WAIT TWO WEEKS TO FIND OUT.

HEY! PARDISSE

I KNEW RIGHT AWAY, BUT I DIDN'T DARE ASK.

IN CLASS, THE TEACHER ASKED US TO WRITE A REPORT ABOUT THE WAR.

IT'S A DIFFICULT SUBJECT, BUT IT CONCERNS US ALL. THINK ABOUT IT CAREFULLY.

I DIDN'T NEED TO DO MUCH THINKING. I KNEW ALL ABOUT THE WAR.

YOU KNOW WHAT YOU'RE GOING TO SAY?

TOTALLY!

I WROTE FOUR PAGES ON THE HISTORICAL CONTEXT ENTITLED "THE ARAB CONQUEST AND OUR WAR."

I WAS VERY PROUD OF MYSELF.

...THIS WAR IS THE SAME AS THE ONE 1400 YEARS AGO...

BUT THE TEACHER DIDN'T SEEM TOO IMPRESSED.

THAT'S PRETTY GOOD. NOW, PARDISSE, COME TO THE BLACKBOARD.

...PARDISSE'S REPORT WAS BY FAR THE BEST. IT WAS A LETTER TO HER FATHER IN WHICH SHE PROMISED TO TAKE CARE OF HER MOTHER AND LITTLE BROTHER.

REST IN PEACE, DAD.

AT RECESS, I TRIED TO CONSOLE HER...

YOUR FATHER ACTED LIKE A GENUINE HERO, YOU SHOULD BE PROUD OF HIM!

I WISH HE WERE ALIVE AND IN JAIL RATHER THAN DEAD AND A HERO.

THOSE WERE HER EXACT WORDS TO ME.

THE JEWELS

YES, IT WAS WAR ALL RIGHT. RIGHT AWAY, THE SUPERMARKETS WERE EMPTY.

I'M NOT SURE IT'S EVEN WORTH GETTING A CART.

I SAW IT FIRST!

LET GO OF THAT!

COME ON, STOP IT!

?

?

MIND YOUR OWN BUSINESS!

WHAT'S HER PROBLEM?

FORGET ABOUT IT, MOM!

IF STORES WERE CLOSED FOR A SINGLE DAY, YOU'D PROBABLY EAT EACH OTHER! AND YOU CALL YOURSELVES CIVILIZED PEOPLE! IF EVERYONE TOOK ONLY WHAT THEY NEEDED THERE WOULD BE ENOUGH TO GO AROUND!

AND IN THE PARKING LOT...

HOW MANY BOXES OF RICE DID WE GET?

UH...TWO!

HMM. WE'LL GO TO THE STORE ACROSS THE STREET AND TRY TO GET MORE. YOU NEVER KNOW!

?

THERE WASN'T MUCH AT THE GAS STATIONS EITHER.

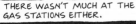

DO YOU HAVE ANY JERRY CANS?

JERRY CANS? WHY?

WHY DO YOU THINK? TO MAKE STRAWBERRY SODA!!!

DON'T TALK TO MY MOTHER LIKE THAT!

EVERY MORNING I HAVE TO DRIVE 40 MILES SO THAT YOU CAN HAVE A PEACEFUL LIFE. HOW AM I GOING TO DO THAT WITH NO CAR? HUH? THAT'S WHY I NEED CANS. FOR GASOLINE! CAN YOU UNDERSTAND THAT? THE CAR RUNS ON GAS!!

LOOK, I AM SO SORRY, DARLING. I'VE BEEN RUNNING AROUND THE WHOLE DAY. I'VE GOT A SPLITTING HEADACHE. YOU KNOW WHAT? I'M JUST GOING TO FILL UP THE TANKS AND THEN WE'LL TRY TO FIND A RESTAURANT.

I HOPE YOU'RE PROUD OF YOURSELF.

AFTER WE MADE UP, WE WENT HOME WITH MY FATHER.

IT TOOK US UNTIL TWO IN THE MORNING. WE OBVIOUSLY DIDN'T GO TO ANY RESTAURANT.

WE DON'T FILL CANS. OTHERWISE THERE WON'T BE ENOUGH FOR EVERYONE.

ALRIGHT. TOO BAD. BUT DO YOU KNOW WHAT'S GOING ON? THE PRESS ISN'T SAYING ANYTHING.

OF COURSE THEY'RE NOT SAYING ANYTHING. IT'S A HUGE MESS!! IRAQ BOMBED THE REFINERY AT ABADAN!

MY GOD! MALI!

OH NO. OH GOD NO.

MALI WAS MY MOTHER'S CHILDHOOD FRIEND. SHE LIVED IN ABADAN WITH HER HUSBAND AND TWO KIDS.

QUICK! CALL THEM!

RING... RING... RING...

NO ONE'S ANSWERING!!

I TRIED HER PLACE TOO, BUT SHE'S DEAF!

DID YOU TRY HER MOTHER? SHE SHOULD KNOW WHAT HAPPENED!

AFTER ABADAN, EVERY BORDER TOWN WAS TARGETED BY BOMBERS. MOST OF THE PEOPLE LIVING IN THOSE AREAS HAD TO FLEE NORTHWARD, FAR FROM THE IRAQI MISSILES.

DING DONG

WHO COULD THAT BE AT THIS HOUR?

I HAVE NO IDEA!

clic!

MALI !!??!

EVERYTHING'S DESTROYED,

HEY, IT'LL BE OK, CALM DOWN...

LOOK AT THIS! THAT'S ALL I COULD SAVE

OH...

C'MON BOYS, I'LL FIX YOU SOME HOT CHOCOLATE.

I DON'T LIKE IT.

ME NEITHER.

FIRST WE WENT TO MY MOTHER'S HOUSE. WE KEPT RINGING THE DOORBELL, BUT SHE'S DEAF. I'M SORRY.

NO, YOU DID THE RIGHT THING COMING HERE.

THAT HOUSE COST A MILLION. A MILLION UP IN SMOKE! CAN YOU IMAGINE THAT?

...

MY FATHER WASN'T SO FOND OF MALI'S HUSBAND. HE THOUGHT HE WAS TOO MATERIALISTIC.

THEY DID HAVE A REALLY NICE HOUSE. WE SPENT OUR VACATION THERE A FEW YEARS EARLIER.

THE MARBLE ALONE COST ME 100,000.

I SEE...

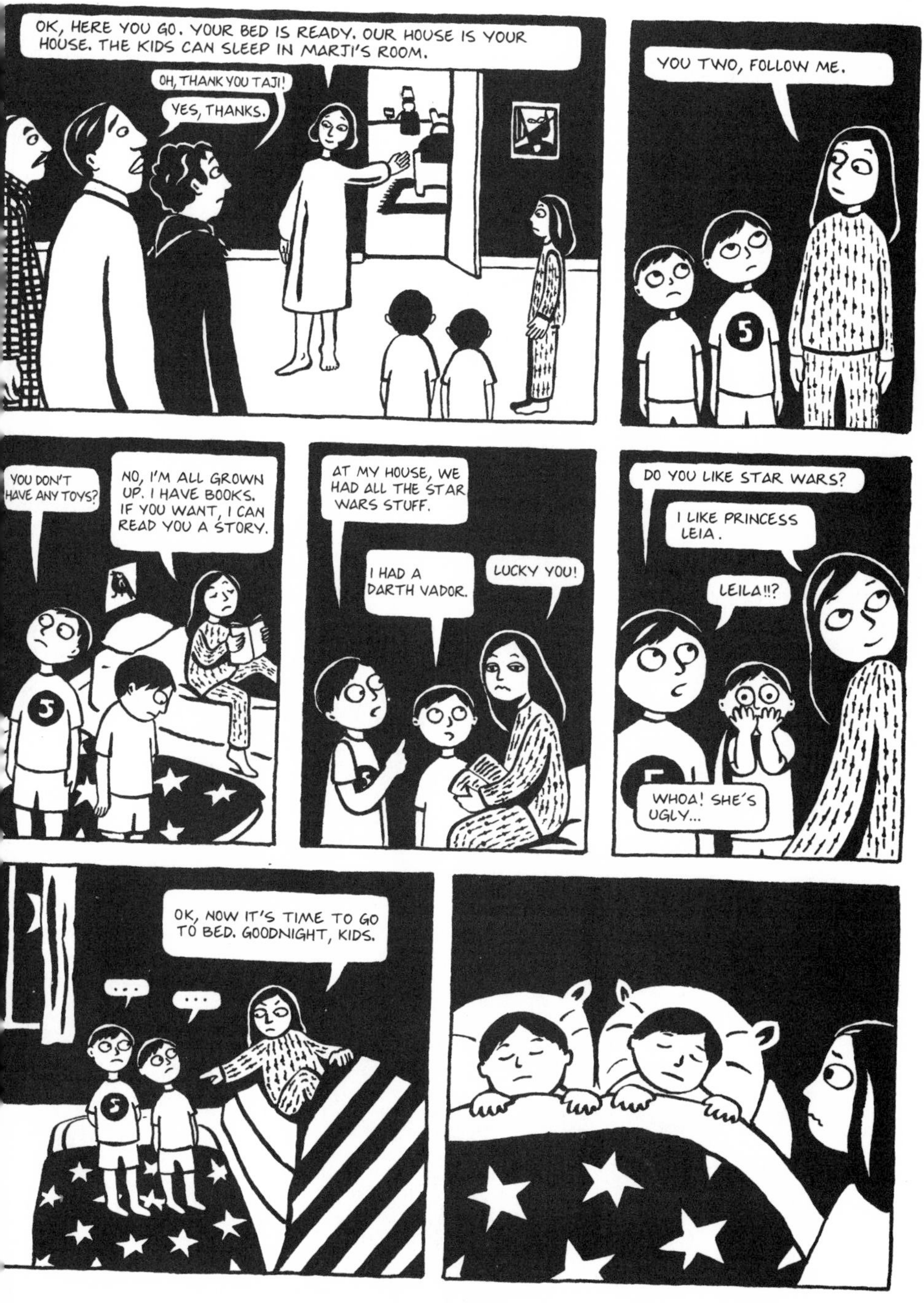
OK, HERE YOU GO. YOUR BED IS READY. OUR HOUSE IS YOUR HOUSE. THE KIDS CAN SLEEP IN MARJI'S ROOM.
OH, THANK YOU TAJI!
YES, THANKS.
YOU TWO, FOLLOW ME.
YOU DON'T HAVE ANY TOYS?
NO, I'M ALL GROWN UP. I HAVE BOOKS. IF YOU WANT, I CAN READ YOU A STORY.
AT MY HOUSE, WE HAD ALL THE STAR WARS STUFF.
I HAD A DARTH VADOR.
LUCKY YOU!
DO YOU LIKE STAR WARS?
I LIKE PRINCESS LEIA.
LEILA!!?
WHOA! SHE'S UGLY...
OK, NOW IT'S TIME TO GO TO BED. GOODNIGHT, KIDS.
...
...

MALI AND HER FAMILY SPENT A WEEK WITH US. THAT'S HOW LONG IT TOOK TO SELL THE JEWELRY AND START OVER AGAIN. MALI'S MOTHER WAS BITTER AND HARD TO DEAL WITH (AND DEAF). BUT THEY WERE HAPPY AT OUR PLACE. THEN, ONE DAY, WE WENT TO THE SUPERMARKET.

GOD, WHAT BRATS!

I WANT THAT!

I WANT THAT OVER THERE!

HEY, THEY STILL HAVE KIDNEY BEANS. WE CAN MAKE CHILI TONIGHT.

OK, WE'LL JUST FORGET ABOUT THE FLATULENCE FACTOR.

WHAT'S FLATULENCE?

WELL... FARTS!

??!

!

HAHAHA! HA HA!

HA HA HA! HA HA HA HA!

SINCE THE REFUGEES HAVE DESCENDED ON TEHRAN, YOU CAN'T GET ANYTHING TO EAT ANYMORE.

YOU'RE RIGHT THERE!

POOPOO!

THEY TAKE EVERYTHING.

MY NEIGHBOR EVEN SAID SHE HEARD THAT THEIR WOMEN ARE PROSTITUTING THEMSELVES. NO DIGNITY AT ALL!

SOON, IT WON'T JUST BE FOOD. WITH ALL THOSE SLUTS OUT THERE, WE'RE GOING TO HAVE TO WATCH OUR HUSBANDS.

ANYWAY, AS EVERYONE KNOWS: "SOUTHERN WOMEN ARE ALL WHORES."

?

IT'S TERRIBLE, WHAT YOU'RE SAYING!

HOW HUMILIATING!

FARTS...

TO HAVE THE IRAQIS ATTACK, AND TO LOSE IN AN INSTANT, EVERYTHING YOU HAD BUILT OVER A LIFETIME, THAT'S ONE THING... BUT TO BE SPAT UPON BY YOUR OWN KIND, IT IS INTOLERABLE!

I FELT SO ASHAMED FOR MYSELF...

?

...AND FELT SO SORRY FOR HER.

THE KEY

THE IRAQI ARMY HAD CONQUERED THE CITY OF KHORRAMSHAHR. THEIR ARMS WERE MODERN, BUT WHERE IRAQ HAD QUALITY, WE HAD QUANTITY. COMPARED TO IRAQ, IRAN HAD A HUGE RESERVOIR OF POTENTIAL SOLDIERS. THE NUMBER OF WAR MARTYRS EMPHASIZED THAT DIFFERENCE.

CAN YOU HELP ME STYLE MY HAIR?

HAVE YOU SEEN ALL THESE CASUALTIES?

HOW CAN I NOT SEE? THEY'RE DOING ALL THEY CAN TO SHOW HOW MANY PEOPLE HAVE DIED. THE STREETS ARE PACKED WITH NUPTIAL CHAMBERS.

ACCORDING TO SHIITE TRADITION, WHEN AN UNMARRIED MAN DIES, A NUPTIAL CHAMBER IS BUILT FOR HIM. THAT WAY, THE DEAD MAN CAN SYMBOLICALLY ATTAIN CARNAL KNOWLEDGE.

IT WAS OBVIOUS THAT MANY OF THE FIGHTERS DIED VIRGINS.

VRUUUUUUU

MOM, DON'T ALL THESE DEAD MEAN ANYTHING TO YOU?

OF COURSE THEY MEAN SOMETHING TO ME! BUT WE ARE STILL LIVING!

OUR COUNTRY HAS ALWAYS KNOWN WAR AND MARTYRS. SO, LIKE MY FATHER SAID: "WHEN A BIG WAVE COMES, LOWER YOUR HEAD AND LET IT PASS!"

THAT'S VERY PERSIAN. T PHILOSOPHY OF RESIGNAT

I AGREED WITH MY MOTHER. I TOO TRIED TO THINK ONLY OF LIFE. HOWEVER, IT WASN'T ALWAYS EASY: AT SCHOOL, THEY LINED US UP TWICE A DAY TO MOURN THE WAR DEAD. THEY PUT ON FUNERAL MARCHES, AND WE HAD TO BEAT OUR BREASTS.

I REMEMBER MY INITIATION. IT WAS THE FIRST DAY OF CLASS AFTER SUMMER VACATION.

WELCOME, GIRLS OF IRAN. THE WAR HAS TAKEN THE FLOWER OF OUR NATION'S YOUTH!

THEN THE LOUDSPEAKERS STARTED TO SING.

BABABABABA♪ ♫ HEY TROOPS OF... BE ♪ READY, ♫ BE READY ♫

? ? ? ?

LET'S GO CHILDREN, ON THE HEART!

WHACK! WHACK!

? ? ? ? ? ?

AND ALL TOGETHER, WE BEGAN THE SESSION.

IT WASN'T AS BAD AS ONE MIGHT THINK. WE'D SEEN IT BEFORE.

HITTING YOURSELF IS ONE OF THE COUNTRY'S RITUALS. DURING CERTAIN RELIGIOUS CEREMONIES, SOME PEOPLE FLAGELLATED THEMSELVES BRUTALLY.

SOMETIMES EVEN WITH CHAINS.

IT COULD GO VERY FAR.

SOMETIMES IT WAS CONSIDERE[D] A MACHO THING.

AFTER A LITTLE WHILE, NO ONE TOOK THE TORTURE SESSIONS SERIOUSLY ANYMORE. AS FOR ME, I IMMEDIATELY STARTED MAKING FUN OF THEM.

THE MARTYRS! THE MARTYRS!

KILL ME!

SATRAPI! WHAT ARE YOU DOING ON THE GROUND?

I'M SUFFERING, CAN'T YOU SEE?

EVERY SITUATION OFFERED AN OPPORTUNITY FOR LAUGHS: LIKE WHEN WE HAD TO KNIT WINTER HOODS FOR THE SOLDIERS...

STOP THAT! OR I'LL CALL THE PRINCIPAL!!

...OR WHEN WE HAD TO DECORATE THE CLASSROOM FOR THE ANNIVERSARY OF THE REVOLUTION...

WHAT ARE THESE GARLANDS?

TOILET PAPER??

YOU'RE AS WORTHLESS AS YOUR DECORATIONS! YOU'RE WORTHLESS!! YOU HEAR ME?! WORTHLESS!!!...

POOPOO

WHO SAID THAT? WHO WAS IT? DOES SHE HAVE THE COURAGE TO STAND UP? IF NOT, YOU'LL ALL BE PUNISHED! WELL? WHO WAS IT ??!!!?

WE WERE COMPLETELY UNITED.

YOU'RE ALL SUSPENDED FOR A WEEK!

I THINK THAT THE REASON WE WERE SO REBELLIOUS WAS THAT OUR GENERATION HAD KNOWN SECULAR SCHOOLS. OBVIOUSLY, THEY CALLED OUR PARENTS IN.

YOUR CHILDREN HAVE NO RESPECT FOR ANYTHING. NO SELF-CONTROL! THE BASIS OF EDUCATION COMES FROM THE FAMILY!

STOP RIGHT THERE. YOU'RE SAYING THAT WE DON'T KNOW HOW TO EDUCATE OUR CHILDREN?

LISTEN, WE'RE AT WAR. A LOT OF CHILDREN DON'T EVEN HAVE SCHOOL THESE DAYS. YOURS HAVE A RARE OPPORTUNITY. SO YOU SHOULD MAKE SURE THEY'RE WELL-BEHAVED!

WELL-BEHAVED? SO THEY CAN HIT THEMSELVES TWICE A DAY??

SO THEY CAN BE COVERED FROM HEAD TO TOE?

SO THAT THEY CAN BE FORBIDDEN TO PLAY LIKE THE KIDS THEY ARE ??

OH!

ANYWAY, THAT'S HOW IT IS! EITHER THEY OBEY THE LAW, OR THEY'RE EXPELLED!!

AND MAKE SURE THEY WEAR THEIR VEILS CORRECTLY...

IF HAIR IS AS STIMULATING AS YOU SAY, THEN YOU NEED TO SHAVE YOUR MUSTACHE!

MY FATHER ACTUALLY SAID THA

GIRLS HAD TO MAKE WINTER HOODS FOR THE SOLDIERS, BUT BOYS HAD TO PREPARE TO BECOME SOLDIERS.

HI MRS. NASRINE. YOU DON'T LOOK WELL.

MRS. NASRINE WAS OUR MAID.

SO, TELL ME, WHAT'S WRONG?

YOU OK?

NO, MY CHILD. I'M NOT OK.

YOU SEE THIS?

IT'S A PLASTIC KEY PAINTED GOLD.

THEY GAVE THIS TO MY SON AT SCHOOL. THEY TOLD THE BOYS THAT IF THEY WENT TO WAR AND WERE LUCKY ENOUGH TO DIE, THIS KEY WOULD GET THEM INTO HEAVEN.

MY GOD!

IT'S OK, CRY, LET YOURSELF GO.

I'LL MAKE SOME TEA.

I'VE SUFFERED SO MUCH. I RAISED MY FIVE KIDS WITH THE WATER OF MY TEARS, NOW THEY WANT TO TRADE THIS KEY FOR MY OLDEST SON...

ALL MY LIFE, I'VE BEEN FAITHFUL TO THE RELIGION. IF IT'S COME TO THIS... WELL, I CAN'T BELIEVE IN ANYTHING ANYMORE...

AND THE CHILD, WHAT DOES HE SAY?

THEY TOLD HIM THAT IN PARA-DISE THERE WILL BE PLENTY OF FOOD, WOMEN AND HOUSES MADE OF GOLD AND DIAMONDS.

WOMEN?

YEAH. WELL, HE'S FOURTEEN YEARS OLD. THAT'S EXCITING.

BRING HIM HERE, I'LL TALK TO HIM.

WELL, I'M OFF TO SCHOOL.

ON THE WAY, I THOUGHT OF MY COUSIN PEYMAN. HE WAS ALSO FOURTEEN.

WHEN I GOT BACK FROM SCHOOL...

LISTEN, CHILD, THOSE ARE JUST MADE-UP STORIES! WHAT HELL? WHAT PARADISE?

HI!

LISTEN INSTEAD OF STUFFING YOUR FACE!

THINK ABOUT WHEN YOU'RE GROWN UP. YOU WILL GO TO COLLEGE. YOU'LL BECOME SOMEBODY.

I'LL MARRY HER!

YOU IDIOT!

STOP, IT'S NO BIG DEAL!

WHAP!

I'M GOING TO MY ROOM.

HEY! PEYMAN?...WHAT?... NEXT WEEK YOU'RE HAVING A PARTY?...I'LL ASK MY MOM.

TELL ME, AT SCHOOL, DID THEY GIVE YOU THE KEYS TO PARADISE?

KEYS TO WHAT?

MOM, PEYMAN INVITED ME TO A PARTY. CAN I GO?

DING DONG

OOOH! SHAHAB!

HEY!

HI!

SHAHAB WAS ANOTHER COUSIN. HE HADN'T BEEN LUCKY: THE WAR STARTED JUST AS HE BEGAN HIS MILITARY SERVICE. THEY SENT HIM TO THE FRONT RIGHT AWAY.

I'M ON LEAVE.

COME IN, COME IN. I'LL MAKE SOME TEA.

I WAS JUST TALKING TO MY MAID. SHE SAID THEY'RE RECRUITING CHILDREN FOR THE FRONT. REALLY!!?

IT'S AWFUL. EVERY DAY I SEE BUSES FULL OF KIDS ARRIVING.

SHIT, YOU SEE THAT?

THEY COME FROM THE POOR AREAS, YOU CAN TELL...FIRST THEY CONVINCE THEM THAT THE AFTERLIFE IS EVEN BETTER THAN DISNEYLAND, THEN THEY PUT THEM IN A TRANCE WITH ALL THEIR SONGS...

IT'S NUTS! THEY HYPNOTIZE THEM AND JUST TOSS THEM INTO BATTLE. ABSOLUTE CARNAGE.

THE KEY TO PARADISE WAS FOR POOR PEOPLE. THOUSANDS OF YOUNG KIDS, PROMISED A BETTER LIFE, EXPLODED ON THE MINEFIELDS WITH THEIR KEYS AROUND THEIR NECKS.

MRS. NASRINE'S SON MANAGED TO AVOID THAT FATE, BUT LOTS OF OTHER KIDS FROM HIS NEIGHBORHOOD DIDN'T

MEANWHILE, I GOT TO GO TO MY FIRST PARTY. NOT ONLY DID MY MOM LET ME GO, SHE ALSO KNITTED ME A SWEATER FULL OF HOLES AND MADE ME A NECKLACE WITH CHAINS AND NAILS. PUNK ROCK WAS IN.

I WAS LOOKING SHARP.

102

THE WINE

AFTER THE BORDER TOWNS, TEHRAN BECAME THE BOMBERS' MAIN TARGET. TOGETHER WITH THE OTHER PEOPLE IN OUR BUILDING, WE TURNED THE BASEMENT INTO A SHELTER. EVERY TIME THE SIREN RANG OUT, EVERYONE WOULD RUN DOWNSTAIRS...

PUT YOUR CIGARETTE OUT. THEY SAY THAT THE GLOW OF A CIGARETTE IS THE EASIEST THING TO SEE FROM THE SKY.

BUT WE'RE IN THE BASEMENT HERE!

AFTER THE BOMBS AND THE INSTINCTIVE FEAR OF DEATH, YOU'D
THINK OF THE VICTIMS AND ANOTHER KIND OF ANXIETY SEIZED Y

IT WASN'T JUST THE BASEMENTS. THE INTERIORS OF HOMES ALSO CHANGED. BUT IT WASN'T ONLY BECAUSE OF THE IRAQI PLANES.

MOM, WHAT'RE YOU DOING?

THE MASKING TAPE IS TO PROTECT AGAINST FLYING GLASS DURING A BOMBING AND THE BLACK CURTAINS ARE TO PROTECT US FROM OUR NEIGHBORS.

WHAT NEIGHBORS?

ACROSS THE STREET. THEY'RE TOTALLY DEVOTED TO THE NEW REGIME. A GLIMPSE OF WHAT GOES ON IN OUR HOUSE WOULD BE ENOUGH FOR THEM TO DENOUNCE US!

YOU KNOW TINOOSH'S DAD?

TINOOSH, YEAH. WHAT ABOUT HIM?

THE OTHER NIGHT, TWO GUARDIANS OF THE REVOLUTION PATROLS PAID THEM A VISIT.

SOMEONE TOLD US YOU WERE PLANNING A PARTY. YOU KNOW THAT IT'S STRICTLY FORBIDDEN!

UM...

..THEY FOUND RECORDS AND VIDEO-CASSETTES AT THEIR PLACE. A DECK OF CARDS, A CHESS SET. IN OTHER WORDS, EVERYTHING THAT'S BANNED.

GET YOUR ASS IN THE CAR. MOVE!

EXCUSE ME, SIR.

SHUT UP, SLUT!

...IT EARNED HIM SEVENTY-FIVE LASHES.

HIS WIFE CRIED SO MUCH THAT THEY FINALLY LET HER OFF WITH A HEFTY FINE. BUT HE CAN'T WALK ANYMORE...NOW YOU SEE WHY I'M PUTTING UP THE CURTAINS. WITH THE PARTIES WE HAVE ON THURSDAYS AND THE CARD GAMES ON MONDAYS, WE HAVE TO BE CAREFUL.

IN SPITE OF ALL THE DANGERS, THE PARTIES WENT ON. "WITHOUT THEM IT WOULDN'T BE PSYCHOLOGICALLY BEARABLE," SOME SAID. "WITHOUT PARTIES, WE MIGHT AS WELL JUST BURY OURSELVES NOW," ADDED THE OTHERS. MY UNCLE INVITED US TO HIS HOUSE TO CELEBRATE THE BIRTH OF MY COUSIN. EVERYONE WAS THERE. EVEN GRANDMA WAS DANCING.

DAMN! POWER OUTAGE!!

BE CAREFUL WHERE YOU STEP!!!

AWWW! NO MORE MUSIC!

DON'T WORRY ABOUT IT! I'LL GO GET THE ZARB.

A ZARB IS A KIND OF DRUM. MY FATHER PLAYED IT VERY WELL. LIKE A PRO.

WE HAD EVERYTHING. WELL, EVERYTHING THAT WAS FORBIDDEN. EVEN ALCOHOL, GALLONS OF IT.

MY UNCLE WAS THE VINTNER. HE HAD BUILT A GENUINE WINE-MAKING LAB IN HIS BASEMENT.

MRS. NASRINE, WHO WAS ALSO HIS CLEANING LADY, CRUSHED THE GRAPES.

GOD FORGIVE ME! GOD FORGIVE ME!

SUDDENLY, SIRENS STARTED TO WAIL...

...AND MY AUNT DID TOO.

IT'S ALRIGHT, STAY CALM!

AAAA...!

I FOUND MYSELF WITH THE NEWBORN BABY WE HAD BEEN CELEBRATING IN MY ARMS.

ER MOTHER HAD ALREADY ABANDONED HER.

SINCE THAT DAY, I'VE HAD DOUBTS ABOUT THE SO-CALLED "MATERNAL INSTINCT."

AFTER THE ALERT, WE WENT HOME.

SHE'S COMPLETELY NUTS! DID YOU SEE HOW SHE DROPPED THE BABY? THAT WAS PRETTY INCREDIBLE!

MY POOR BROTHER ISN'T EXACTLY SPOILED.

HALT!

HALT!

OPEN THE DOOR AND GET OUT!

ID, REGISTRATION AND DRIVER'S LICENSE.

OK. OK.

GO AHHH.

AHH...

BEEN DRINKING, HAVE WE!!?!!

NO, ABSOLUTELY NOT!

YOU THINK I'M STUPID?!!!... I CAN TELL BY YOUR TIE! PIECE OF WESTERNIZED TRASH!

I WON'T TAKE THAT FROM YOU. FOR TWENTY YEARS I'VE WORKED FOR THIS COUNTRY AND YOU DARE TO TALK TO ME LIKE THAT?

FORGIVE HIM

SHUT UP

FORGIVE HIM. LISTEN, I COULD BE YOUR MOTHER. HOW OLD ARE YOU? SIXTEEN?... MY DAUGHTER IS TWELVE... FORGIVE HIM...

YOU'RE LUCKY TO HAVE THIS WOMAN FOR YOUR WIFE, OTHERWISE YOU'D ALREADY BE IN HELL!

THANKS, THANKS SO MUCH!

YOU SAY YOU HAVEN'T BEEN DRINKING. WE'RE GOING TO SEE WHAT YOU HAVE AT HOME.

GRANDMA! MARJI! WHEN WE'RE HOME, GET OUT FIRST. I'LL TRY TO STALL HIM. FLUSH ALL THE ALCOHOL DOWN THE TOILET.

BUT HOW?

DON'T WORRY DEAR. I'M USED TO IT. WHEN YOUR FATHER WAS ALIVE, I WAS ALWAYS HIDING HIS TRACTS.

THEY FOLLOWED US ALL THE WAY HOME.

MUST YOU REALLY COME UPSTAIRS? OUR ELDERY NEIGHBOR HAS A HEART CONDITION. IF HE'S FRIGHTENED BY THE NOISE, IT COULD KILL HIM.

HURRY UP!

WHERE DO YOU TWO THINK YOU'RE GOING?

I HAVE DIABETES, MY BOY. IF I DON'T DRINK A LITTLE SYRUP, I'M GOING TO FAINT.

DIABETES, JUST LIKE MY MOTHER!

SO YOU UNDERSTAND IT'S URGENT!

GO AHEAD.

IT WAS A MIRACLE.

HURRY UP! I DON'T KNOW HOW MUCH LONGER YOUR FATHER CAN STALL THEM!

HURRY! HURRY!

AND THE FINAL TOUCH.

CLICK!

HERE THEY COME

WHERE'S THE GUY?

WHERE INDEED! THEIR FAITH HAS NOTHING TO DO WITH IDEOLOGY! A FEW BILLS WERE ALL HE NEEDED TO FORGET THE WHOLE THING!!

HEY, YOU DIDN'T THROW IT ALL OUT?

YEP

NO MORE?

NOPE

MY GOD!...I NEED A PICK-ME-UP...

THE CIGARETTE

THE WAR HAD BEEN GOING ON FOR TWO YEARS. WE WERE USED TO IT. I WAS GROWING UP AND I EVEN HAD FRIENDS OLDER THAN ME.

YESTERDAY ON THE NEWS THEY SAID WE DESTROYED 13 IRAQI PLANES. RIGHT AFTER ON THE BBC, I HEARD THAT IN FACT THE IRAQIS HAD SHOT DOWN TWO OF OURS.

IT'S PERFECTLY CLEAR. EVERY DAY THEY TELL US THAT WE'VE DESTROYED TEN PLANES AND FIVE TANKS. IF YOU START FROM THE BEGINNING OF THE WAR, THAT MAKES SIX THOUSAND PLANES AND THREE THOUSAND TANKS DESTROYED. EVEN THE AMERICANS DON'T HAVE AN ARMY THIS BIG.

I GET IT. I'M GOING TO TELL MY DAD THAT ONE.

?

BRINGGG...

HEY, THERE'S THE BELL. DON'T YOU HAVE CLASS?

NO, WE'VE GOT PHYSICAL EDUCA-TION BUT WE'RE NOT GOING. WE'RE GOING FOR BURGERS.

BURGERS?

THEY ALSO HAVE HOT DOGS.

ALL YOU NEEDED WAS SOME MONEY.

YEAH! AT KANSAS ON JORDAN AVENUE.

DON'T LOOK AT ME LIKE THAT. WE'LL CLIMB THE WALL.

THE WALL??!!

HA HA HA HA! HA HA HA!

!!

IF I WANTED TO BE FRIENDS WITH 14-YEAR-OLDS, I HAD TO DO IT.

I WASN'T CHICKEN, SO I FOLLOWED THEM.

I HAD ALREADY BROKEN THE RULES ONCE BY GOING TO THE DEMONSTRATION IN '79. THIS WAS THE SECOND TIME.

JORDAN AVENUE WAS WHERE THE TEENAGERS FROM NORTH TEHRAN (THE NICE NEIGHBORHOODS) HUNG OUT. KANSAS WAS ITS TEMPLE.

IF SOME PUBLIC PLACES HAD SURVIVED THE REGIME'S REPRESSION, EITHER IT WAS TO LEAVE US A LITTLE FREE SPACE, OR ELSE IT WAS OUT OF IGNORANCE. PERSONALLY, THE LATTER THEORY SOUNDED MORE LIKELY. THEY PROBABLY HADN'T THE SLIGHTEST IDEA WHAT "KANSAS" WAS.

DID YOU SEE HIS HAIR? JUST LIKE ROD STEWART!

STOP

KAN

YEAH, IF HE GETS CAUGHT, HE'LL GET A BUZZ CUT!

...IN SPITE OF EVERYTHING, KIDS WERE TRYING TO LOOK HIP, EVEN UNDER RISK OF ARRES

MY FRIENDS WEREN'T ACTUALLY THAT INTERESTED IN THE HAMBURGERS...

WC

WE LET THE BOYS KNOW THAT THEY COULD FOLLOW US BY A FEW SIGNS.

FOLLOW THE OTHERS, I MEAN. I WA TOO YOUNG TO INTEREST THEM.

wooooo

...THE SIRENS WENT OFF.

WHAT THE HELL ARE YOU DOING??

HIT THE DIRT!

?

?

?

WE HAD BEEN TOLD THAT IF WE WERE IN THE STREET DURING A BOMBING, WE SHOULD LIE DOWN IN THE GUTTER FOR SAFETY.

HA! YOU CHICKEN!

THE WONDERFUL DAY WAS SPOILED BY MY MOM.

SO HOW WAS SCHOOL?

OK. WHY?

YOU DARE TO LIE STRAIGHT TO MY FACE?

I'M NOT LYING!

SO MAYBE IT'S ME WHO CUT CLASS?

WHAT CLASS?

YOU TELL ME THE TRUTH RIGHT NOW OR ELSE YOU'LL BE PUNISHED TWICE!

MY MOTHER USED THE SAME TACTICS AS THE TORTURERS.

BUT ALL I HAD WAS RELIGION CLASS!

I DON'T GIVE A DAMN! YOU DON'T CUT CLASS!

AND YOU JUST LIED AGAIN! THE SCHOOL CALLED AND SAID YOU HAD GRAMMAR THIS AFTERNOON!

I HAD SAID RELIGION TO TRY TO MAKE MY MOTHER LESS ANGRY, BUT IT HADN'T WORKED.

THIS TIME I COVERED FOR YOU, BUT IT'S THE LAST TIME! NOW IS THE TIME FOR LEARNING. YOU HAVE YOUR WHOLE LIFE TO HAVE FUN! WHAT ARE YOU GOING TO BE WHEN YOU GROW UP?? IN THIS COUNTRY YOU HAVE TO KNOW EVERYTHING BETTER THAN ANYONE ELSE IF YOU'RE GOING TO SURVIVE!!

DIDN'T YOU MEET DAD WHEN YOU WERE FOURTEEN?

YOU'RE NOT FOURTEEN!

SO? I'M TWELVE!

DICTATOR! YOU ARE THE GUARDIAN OF THE REVOLUTION OF THIS HOUSE!

SOMEWHAT LATER...

THE IRANIAN ARMY HAS RETAKEN KHORRAMSHAHR...

...FOR THE FOURTH TIME THIS MONTH.

EVEN IF IT'S TRUE, WHAT DIFFERENCE DOES IT MAKE TO US?

MAY I GO TO THE BASEMENT, MA'AM?

YES, MISS SATRAPI.

THE BASEMENT WAS MY HIDEAWAY.

CLICK

AS IT TURNED OUT, THEY DID RETAKE KHORRAMSHAHR. WE ALL THOUGHT THAT THE WAR WOULD FINALLY END.

IN FACT, IRAQ PROPOSED A SETTLEMENT, AND SAUDI ARABIA WAS WILLING TO PAY FOR RECONSTRUCTION, TO RESTORE PEACE TO THE AREA.

BUT OUR GOVERNMENT WAS AGAINST IT.

THEY DECLARED:

WE REFUSE THIS IMPOSED PEACE!

WE SHALL CONQUER KARBALA*!

✣ A SHIITE HOLY CITY IN IRAQ

SO WE PLUNGED DEEPER INTO WAR...

THE WALLS WERE SUDDENLY COVERED WITH BELLIGERENT SLOGANS.

THE ONE THAT STRUCK ME MOST BY ITS GORY IMAGERY WAS: "TO DIE A MARTYR IS TO INJECT BLOOD INTO THE VEINS OF SOCIETY."

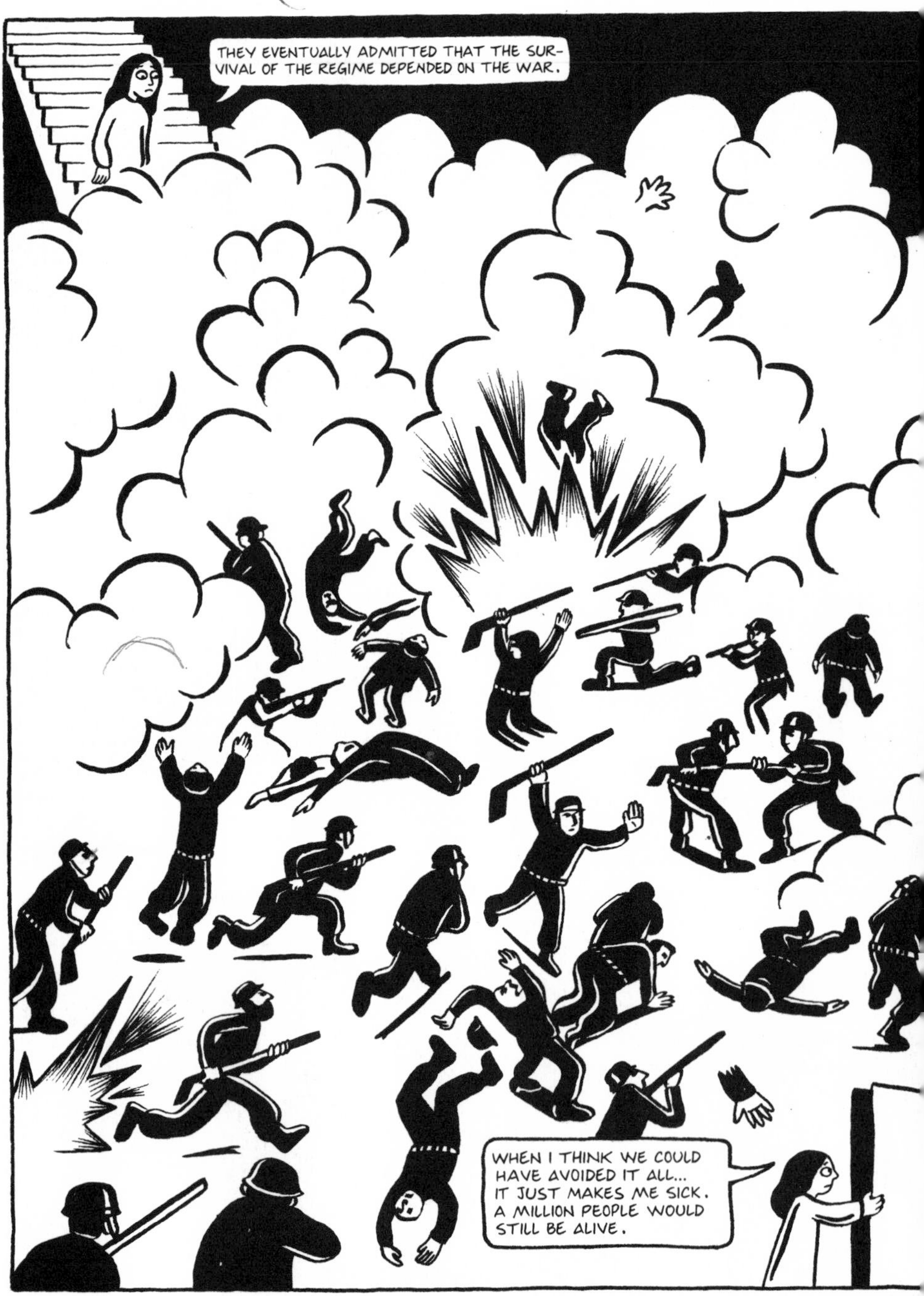
THEY EVENTUALLY ADMITTED THAT THE SURVIVAL OF THE REGIME DEPENDED ON THE WAR.
WHEN I THINK WE COULD HAVE AVOIDED IT ALL... IT JUST MAKES ME SICK. A MILLION PEOPLE WOULD STILL BE ALIVE.

NATURALLY, THE REGIME BECAME MORE REPRESSIVE.

IN THE NAME OF THAT WAR, THEY EXTERMINATED THE ENEMY WITHIN.

THOSE WHO OPPOSED THE REGIME WERE SYSTEMATICALLY ARRESTED...

AND EXECUTED TOGETHER.

AS FOR ME, I SEALED MY ACT OF REBELLION AGAINST MY MOTHER'S DICTATORSHIP BY SMOKING THE CIGARETTE I'D STOLEN FROM MY UNCLE TWO WEEKS EARLIER.

KOFFF! KOFFF! KOFFF!!!

IT WAS AWFUL. BUT THIS WAS NOT THE MOMENT TO GIVE IN.

WITH THIS FIRST CIGARETTE, I KISSED CHILDHOOD GOODBYE.

NOW I WAS A GROWN-UP.

THE PASSPORT

JULY 1982. WE WERE AT MY AUNT'S PLACE. THE INTERNAL WAR HAD BECOME A BIGGER ISSUE THAN THE WAR AGAINST IRAQ. ANYONE SHOWING THE SLIGHTEST RESISTANCE TO THE REGIME WAS PERSECUTED.

THERE MUST BE A LOT OF PEOPLE IN THE OPPOSITION IN OUR NEIGHBORHOOD. WE HEAR GUNSHOTS EVERY DAY.

TAHER, STOP SMOKING!

THE STRESS I GET FROM EVERY GUNSHOT I HEAR IS MUCH WORSE FOR ME THAN THE CIGARETTES.

SINCE HE HAD SENT HIS OLDEST SON TO HOLLAND, UNCLE TAHER HAD HAD TWO HEART ATTACKS. HE WAS ABSOLUTELY FORBIDDEN TO SMOKE.

THE BUTCHER TOLD ME HE'S SEEN KIDS EXECUTED IN THE STREET WITHOUT EVEN HAVING BEEN JUDGED. THE SHAME OF IT.

WHEN I THINK ABOUT IT, I'M GLAD THAT MY SON IS SAFELY ABROAD. BUT WITH THE BORDERS CLOSED, HOW AM I EVER GOING TO SEE HIM AGAIN?

THE BORDERS WERE CLOSED FOR THREE YEARS BETWEEN 1980 AND 1983.

HOW MANY TIMES DID I SAY TO MY WIFE, "COME ON, LET'S JOIN HIM." SHE DIDN'T WANT TO. SHE INVOKED HER COUNTRY, HER FAMILY, ETC, ETC.

ANYWAY, I'M ALREADY 59. BUT THOSE POOR 20-YEAR-OLDS WHO GET SLAUGHTERED. THEY KILL ME... THEY KILL ME!

MY UNCLE TAHER WAS SO SAD THAT IT HURT TO LOOK AT HIM. NO ONE DARED SAY A WORD.

SOME DAYS LATER .

WHAT ARE YOU THINKING?

ABOUT TAHER. HIS SON LEAVING HAS DONE HIM IN. I'VE NEVER SEEN HIM LIKE THAT.

CAN YOU IMAGINE? A THIRTEEN, FOURTEEN-YEAR-OLD CHILD, ALONE IN A COUNTRY WHERE HE DOESN'T EVEN SPEAK THE LANGUAGE?

TCH...AT FOURTEEN YOU DON'T NEED YOUR PARENTS ANYMORE!

GET REAL. UP TO A CERTAIN AGE, YOU NEED YOUR PARENTS, THEN LATER, THEY NEED YOU.

?

YOU'D BE BETTER OFF WITHOUT NAIL POLISH. YOU COULD GET ARRESTED.

I'LL PUT MY HANDS IN MY POCKETS.

PRETTY STUBBORN GIRL, HUH?

WHERE DO YOU SUPPOSE SHE GETS THAT?

SOMETIMES IT SCARES ME HOW BLUNT SHE IS.

IT'LL HELP HER LATER ON. YOU'LL SEE.

AM SO LUCKY TO BE MARRIED TO A MAN LIKE YOU. YOU'RE SO SENSITIVE. THE INDEST MAN ON EARTH.

HOW CAN YOU BE INSENSI-TIVE TO THE WOMAN YOU LOVE?

RRING... RRING...

IT ALWAYS RINGS AT THE WRONG TIME !

GOOD LORD, AGAIN !

WHAT?

UNCLE TAHER HAD JUST SUFFERED HIS THIRD HEART ATTACK. WE WERE OFF TO THE HOSPITAL.

RED CRESCENT TRUCKS WERE PULLED UP IN FRONT OF THE HOSPITAL, CALLING FOR PEOPLE TO GIVE BLOOD FOR THE WAR WOUNDED. THERE WERE SO MANY OF THEM.

GIVE BLOOD! GIVE BLOOD!!

GIVE BLOOD!

I FELT BOTH ANGRY AND EMBARRASSED...

ONCE INSIDE THE HOSPITAL I FELT EVEN WORSE.

I'M LOOKING FOR MR. TALISCHI'S ROOM.

TALISCHI...THAT'S 342, THIRD FLOOR, AT THE END OF THE HALL TO THE RIGHT.

342

THEY THREW A GRENADE...THEY WANTED TO ARREST SOME COMMUNISTS WHO WERE HIDING NEAR OUR PLACE, AND THEY THREW A GRENADE...TAHER COULDN'T DEAL WITH IT... WHEN I CAME INTO THE LIVING ROOM, HE WAS LYING ON THE FLOOR...

SHHH

342

HE NEEDS OPEN HEART SURGERY, BUT THEY'RE NOT EQUIPPED HERE. THEY TOLD ME THAT HE HAS TO BE SENT TO ENGLAND.

TO DO THAT, HE NEEDS A PERMIT. THEY GAVE ME THE NAME OF THE HOSPITAL DIRECTOR. IF HE AGREES, TAHER WILL GET A PASSPORT SO HE CAN GO.

SINCE THE BORDERS WERE CLOSED, ONLY VERY SICK PEOPLE (IF THEY GOT A PERMIT FROM THE HEALTH MINISTRY) WERE ALLOWED TO LEAVE.

IT'S ON THE 4TH FLOOR, NUMBER 406.

NLY MY AUNT WAS ALLOWED IN. SHE AD A BIG SURPRISE. THE DIRECTOR AS HER FORMER WINDOW WASHER. E ACTED AS IF SHE DIDN'T RECOGNIZE M TO AVOID OFFENDING HIM.

MY HUSBAND HAD HIS THIRD EART ATTACK. HE NEEDS MEDI-AL CARE OUTSIDE THE COUNTRY.

HMM...

WE'LL DO OUR BEST. IF GOD WILLS IT, HE'LL GET BETTER. EVERYTHING DEPENDS ON GOD.

I NEED YOUR AUTHORIZATION SO HE CAN GET A PASSPORT !

IF GOD WILLS IT.

ALL THAT CREEPY WINDOW WASHER HAD TO DO TO BECOME DIRECTOR OF THE HOSPITAL WAS TO GROW A BEARD AND PUT ON A SUIT ! THE FATE OF MY HUSBAND DEPENDS ON A WINDOW WASHER ! NOW HE'S SO RELIGIOUS THAT HE WON'T LOOK A WOMAN IN THE EYE. THE PATHETIC FOOL !

AFTER THE DIRECTOR, WE WENT TO SEE THE CHIEF OF STAFF, DR. FATHI.

MA'AM, WE WILL DO WHAT WE CAN. WE ARE TERRIBLY STRAPPED AT THE MOMENT.

LOOK IN THIS ROOM. THEY'RE ALL VICTIMS OF CHEMICAL WEAPONS!

THE GERMANS SELL CHEMICAL WEAPONS TO IRAN AND IRAQ. THE WOUNDED ARE THEN SENT TO GERMANY TO BE TREATED. VERITABLE HUMAN GUINEA PIGS.

WHY ARE YOU TELLING ME THIS?! I COULDN'T CARE LESS. I WANT MY HUSBAND TO GET WELL!

CALM DOWN

CALM DOWN, DEAR. EVERYTHING WILL BE ALL RIGHT. DON'T WORRY.

WE'LL BE RIGHT BACK!

WE WENT TO SEE AN ACQUAIN-
TANCE OF MY FATHER'S, KHOSRO.
HIS BROTHER AND MY UNCLE ANOOSH
WERE IN PRISON TOGETHER DURING
THE REIGN OF THE SHAH.

EBI, THE BROTHER OF
ANOOSH? COME IN! COME IN!

SINCE THEY SHUT DOWN MY
PUBLISHING COMPANY, I'VE BEEN
PRINTING FAKE PASSPORTS. BIG
SELLERS. YOU WANT ONE?

NOT ME, MY
BROTHER-IN-LAW.

WHEN THEY LET HIM OUT, MY
BROTHER STARTED GOING TO
COUNTER-REVOLUTIONARY
DEMONSTRATIONS. HE TOLD ME THAT
THE CHIEF OF THE NEW EXECUTIONERS
WAS HIS TORTURER IN THE SHAH'S
PRISON. HE SAW IT WITH HIS OWN
EYES. HE SAID "KHOSRO, I CAN'T
TAKE ANY MORE." I MADE HIM A
FAKE PASSPORT AND HE SOUGHT
POLITICAL ASYLUM IN SWEDEN.

LOOK, EBI, A WHOLE MONTH'S
WORK, JUST FOR THE STAMP.

HOW MUCH TIME
WILL IT TAKE TO
MAKE A PASSPORT?

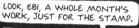

A WEEK.

CRR...

YOU CAN COME IN.
THEY'RE FRIENDS.

THIS IS NILOUFAR. HER BROTHER
WAS MY MESSENGER BOY. THEY
ARE LOOKING ALL OVER FOR HER
BECAUSE SHE'S A COMMUNIST. I
LET HER STAY IN MY BASEMENT.

SHE'S EIGHTEEN, THE SAME AGE
AS MY DAUGHTER, MANDANA.

KHOSRO'S DAUGHTER HAD LEFT
WITH HER MOTHER RIGHT
AFTER THE REVOLUTION.

THEY'VE BEEN SEARCHING
THE HOUSES OF EVERYONE
IN HER FAMILY. THIS IS THE
ONLY PLACE SHE'S SAFE.

AFTER NEGOTIATING A PRICE, THE EQUIVALENT OF ABOUT $200, KHOSRO AGREED TO MAKE A PASSPORT IN FIVE DAYS. WE WENT BACK TO THE HOSPITAL FEELING A LITTLE BETTER.

SO?

I SAW KHOSRO. HE CAN MAKE A PASSPORT FOR TAHER BY WEDNESDAY.

HE'S COME TO. HE WANTS TO SEE YOU.

SEE, IT'S NOT THE CIGARETTES THAT DID IT! IT WAS THAT DAMN GRENADE...

DON'T UPSET YOUR-SELF, TALK ABOUT SOMETHING ELSE.

LOOK AT HOW LITTLE MARJI IS GROWING UP. ONE DAY SHE'LL LEAVE AND YOU'LL SEE HOW HARD IT IS TO LOSE YOUR KIDS.

I HAVE ONLY ONE WISH, AND THAT'S TO SEE MY SON AGAIN, ONE LAST TIME.

TWO DAYS LATER, NILOUFAR, THE EIGHTEEN-YEAR-OLD COMMUNIST, WAS SPOTTED.

ARRESTED...

AND EXECUTED.

CHOSRO FOUND HIS HOUSE RANSACKED...

FLED ACROSS THE MOUNTAINS TO TURKEY...

AND SOUGHT ASYLUM WITH HIS BROTHER IN SWEDEN.

HE NEVER GOT TO MAKE THE PASSPORT.

THREE WEEKS AFTER THESE EVENTS, UNCLE TAHER WAS BURIED. HIS REAL PASSPORT ARRIVED THE SAME DAY...

...HE NEVER GOT TO SEE HIS SON...

KIM WILDE

A YEAR AFTER MY UNCLE DIED, THE BORDERS WERE REOPENED. MY PARENTS RAN TO GET PASSPORTS.

LOOK AT THE LAST PAGE: "IT IS STRICTLY FORBIDDEN TO TRAVEL IN OCCUPIED PALESTINE WITH THIS DOCUMENT."

MY GOD. JUST LOOK AT ME IN THIS PICTURE, WITH THE SCARF ON MY HEAD.

CAN I SEE?

SHE SURE DIDN'T LOOK VERY HAPPY. IN FACT, SHE WAS UNRECOGNIZABLE.

AS SOON AS I GET MY PASSPORT, WE'LL GO ON A BIG TRIP!

WELL, ACTUALLY...

WE WANT TO SPEND SOME TIME TOGETHER, JUST THE TWO OF US, FOR A FEW DAYS.

WHERE?

TURKEY.

BAH...TURKEY'S FOR THE BIRDS. ONLY UNCOOL PEOPLE GO TO TURKEY. IF YOU'RE TAKING A TRIP, WHY NOT GO TO EUROPE OR THE UNITED STATES?!...

IF YOU WANT US TO BRING YOU BACK SOME PRESENTS, JUST ASK.

WHAT CAN YOU BRING ME BACK FROM TURKEY? SHISH-KEBABS?

LISTEN MARJI, WHERE DO YOU THINK ALL THE HIP STUFF YOU LIKE COMES FROM?

DURING THE WAR, THERE WERE NO IMPORTS FROM THE WEST.

A DENIM JACKET, CHOCOLATE, A POSTER, NO, TWO POSTERS. ONE OF KIM WILDE AND ONE OF IRON MAIDEN.

IRON MAIDEN? THOSE FOUR BRUTES?

THEY'RE NOT BRUTES. I REALLY LIKE WHAT THEY DO.

YOU LIKE THAT?

I LOVE IT.

SEE, MOM?

FIRST THING AFTER THEY GOT TO ISTANBUL, THEY WENT TO BUY THE POSTERS.

I'M GLAD WE FOUND JUST WHAT SHE WANTED!

ABSOLUTELY! IT'S SO HARD FOR KIDS IN IRAN. THE POOR THINGS.

TELL ME THE TRUTH, YOU REALLY LIKE IRON MAIDEN?

YOU HYPOCRITE!

ABSOLUTELY!

I WONDER HOW WE'RE GOING TO GET THEM PAST CUSTOMS!

I'VE BEEN WONDERING MYSELF. THEY'RE ENORMOUS.

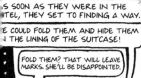

S SOON AS THEY WERE IN THE ͗TEL, THEY SET TO FINDING A WAY.

E COULD FOLD THEM AND HIDE THEM ͟ THE LINING OF THE SUITCASE!

FOLD THEM? THAT WILL LEAVE MARKS. SHE'LL BE DISAPPOINTED.

WE COULD JUST CARRY THEM UNDER OUR ARMS AND ACT NATURAL.

UNDER OUR ARMS? COME ON!

AND THEN MY MOTHER HAD A GREAT IDEA...

TAKE OFF YOUR COAT.

HEY, WHAT ARE YOU DOING?

WAIT, YOU'LL SEE.

CRRAK

SHE TORE OUT THE LINING.

THEN, SHE PLACED THE TWO POSTERS BEHIND IT...

...AND THEN SEWED IT BACK IN.

YOU'RE SURE I LOOK NORMAL?

YOU JUST LOOK LIKE YOU'RE WEARING SHOULDER PADS. IT'S STYLISH.

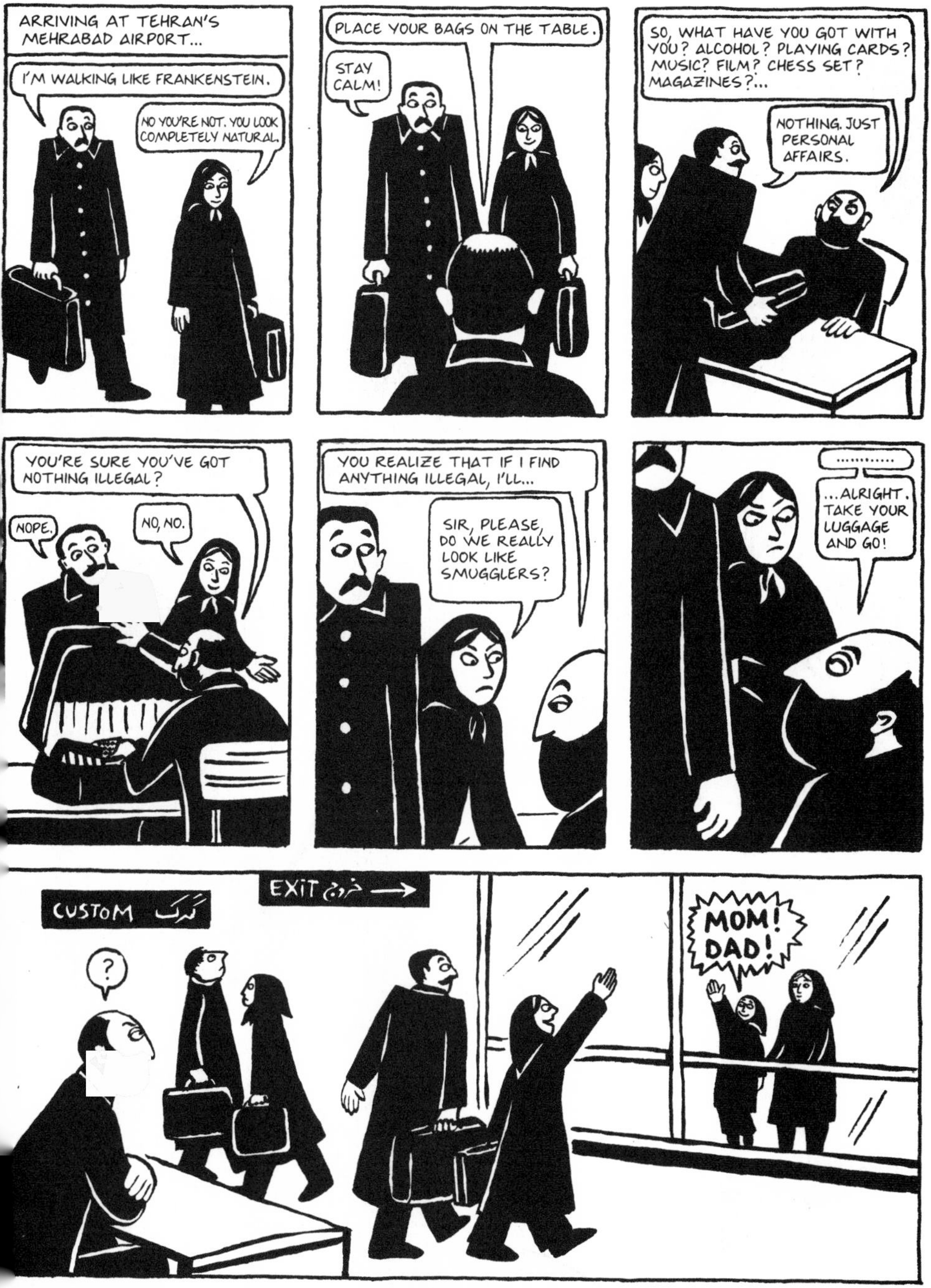
ARRIVING AT TEHRAN'S MEHRABAD AIRPORT...
I'M WALKING LIKE FRANKENSTEIN.
NO YOU'RE NOT. YOU LOOK COMPLETELY NATURAL.
PLACE YOUR BAGS ON THE TABLE.
STAY CALM!
SO, WHAT HAVE YOU GOT WITH YOU? ALCOHOL? PLAYING CARDS? MUSIC? FILM? CHESS SET? MAGAZINES?...
NOTHING. JUST PERSONAL AFFAIRS.
YOU'RE SURE YOU'VE GOT NOTHING ILLEGAL?
NOPE.
NO, NO.
YOU REALIZE THAT IF I FIND ANYTHING ILLEGAL, I'LL...
SIR, PLEASE, DO WE REALLY LOOK LIKE SMUGGLERS?
....
...ALRIGHT. TAKE YOUR LUGGAGE AND GO!
CUSTOM گمرک
EXIT خروج
?
MOM! DAD!

BACK HOME...

HERE. THIS IS FOR YOU. NIKE'S LATEST MODEL.

AND THIS...

WOW! MICHAEL JACKSON!

AND HERE'S YOUR DENIM JACKET.

COOL!

WHAT ABOUT MY POSTERS?

EBI! BRING YOUR COAT!

BE CAREFUL!

I WANTED POSTERS, NOT PHOTOS!!

YOU JUST WAIT!

CRRAK

FAR OUT!!

DAD, YOU'RE A GENIUS!

THANK YOUR MOTHER. IT WAS HER IDEA.

!!

THANK YOU MOM! SO, HOW WAS TURKEY?

GREAT! IT WAS A LITTLE COLD, BUT IT WAS NICE.

I LOVED TURKEY.

I PUT MY POSTERS UP IN MY ROOM.

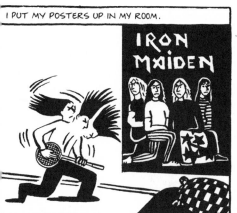

I PUT MY 1983 NIKES ON...

...AND MY DENIM JACKET WITH THE MICHAEL JACKSON BUTTON, AND OF COURSE, MY HEADSCARF.

SO WHAT DO YOU THINK?

NICE! VERY CUTE!

OK, I'M GOING OUT.

WHERE?

TO BUY SOME TAPES.

WHERE?

NOT FAR. ON GANDHI AVENUE.

BE BACK IN AN HOUR!

I'LL BE BACK IN TWO HOURS.

FOR AN IRANIAN MOTHER, MY MOM WAS VERY PERMISSIVE. I ONLY KNEW TWO OR THREE OTHER GIRLS WHO COULD GO OUT ALONE AT THIRTEEN.

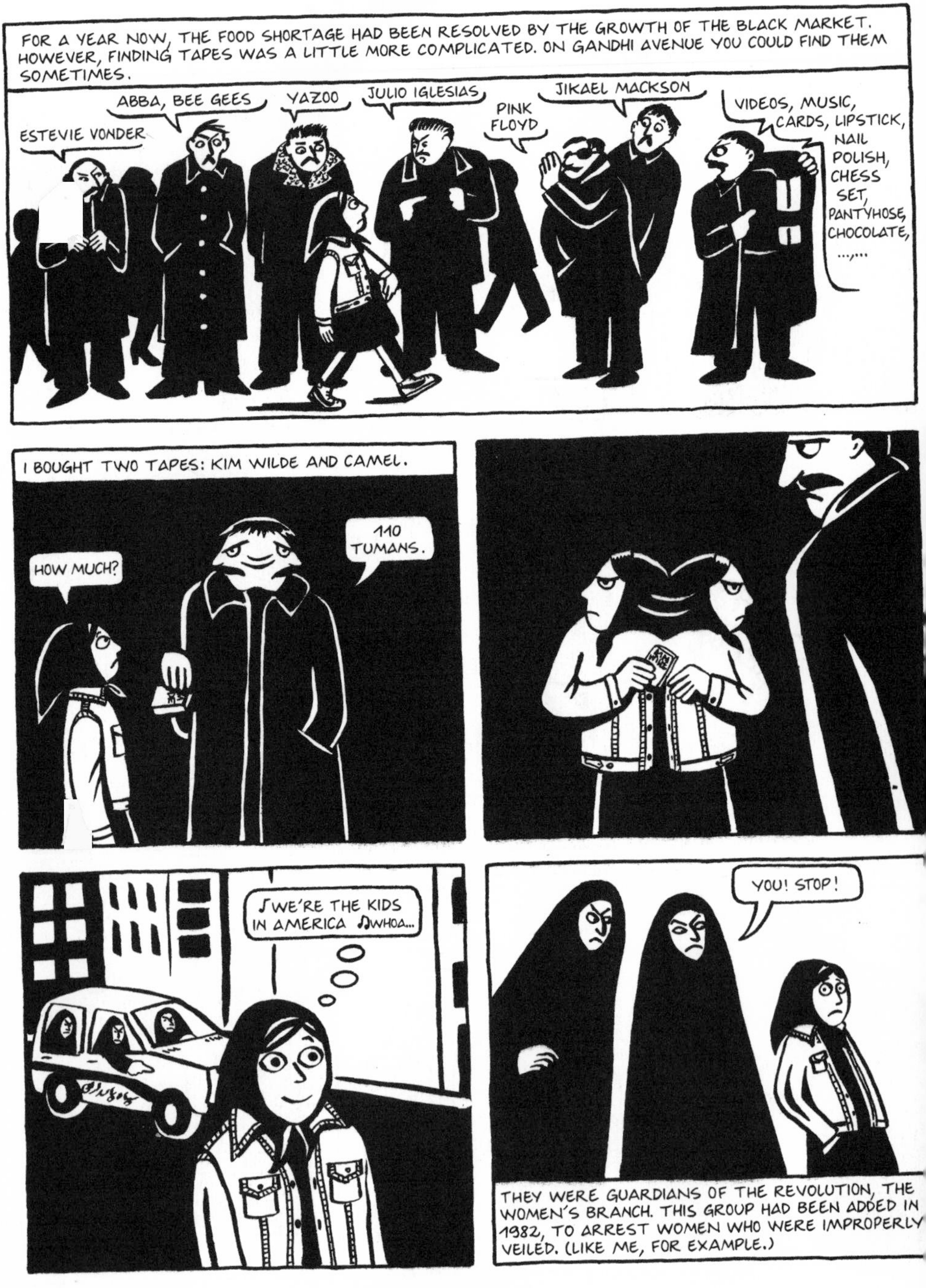
FOR A YEAR NOW, THE FOOD SHORTAGE HAD BEEN RESOLVED BY THE GROWTH OF THE BLACK MARKET. HOWEVER, FINDING TAPES WAS A LITTLE MORE COMPLICATED. ON GANDHI AVENUE YOU COULD FIND THEM SOMETIMES.
ESTEVIE VONDER
ABBA, BEE GEES
YAZOO
JULIO IGLESIAS
PINK FLOYD
JIKAEL MACKSON
VIDEOS, MUSIC, CARDS, LIPSTICK, NAIL POLISH, CHESS SET, PANTYHOSE, CHOCOLATE, ...,...
I BOUGHT TWO TAPES: KIM WILDE AND CAMEL.
HOW MUCH?
110 TUMANS.
♪WE'RE THE KIDS IN AMERICA ♫WHOA...
YOU! STOP!
THEY WERE GUARDIANS OF THE REVOLUTION, THE WOMEN'S BRANCH. THIS GROUP HAD BEEN ADDED IN 1982, TO ARREST WOMEN WHO WERE IMPROPERLY VEILED. (LIKE ME, FOR EXAMPLE.)

THEIR JOB WAS TO PUT US BACK ON THE STRAIGHT AND NARROW BY EXPLAINING THE DUTIES OF MUSLIM WOMEN.

WHY ARE YOU WEARING THOSE "PUNK" SHOES?

WHAT PUNK SHOES?

THOSE!

BUT THESE ARE SNEAKERS!

SHUT UP! THEY'RE PUNK.

IT WAS OBVIOUS THAT SHE HAD NO IDEA WHAT PUNK WAS.

THERE WAS NO ALTERNATIVE. I HAD TO LIE.

I WEAR THESE BECAUSE I PLAY BASKETBALL.

I'M ON MY SCHOOL'S TEAM.

OH SURE. I CAN TELL BY YOUR HEIGHT!

AND YOU WEAR THIS JACKET FOR BASKETBALL TOO??

WHAT DO I SEE HERE? MICHAEL JACKSON! THAT SYMBOL OF DECADENCE?

NO, IT'S MALCOLM X, THE LEADER OF BLACK MUSLIMS IN AMERICA.

DON'T GIVE ME THAT! IT'S MICHAEL JACKSON!

WHO? I DON'T KNOW HIM.

BACK THEN, MICHAEL JACKSON WAS STILL BLACK.

LOWER YOUR SCARF, YOU LITTLE WHORE!

AREN'T YOU ASHAMED TO WEAR TIGHT JEANS LIKE THESE??

THEY SHRANK!!

GO ON, GET IN THE CAR. WE'RE TAKING YOU DOWN TO THE COMMITTEE.

THE COMMITTEE WAS THE HQ OF THE GUARDIANS OF THE REVOLUTION.

AT THE COMMITTEE, THEY DIDN'T HAVE TO INFORM MY PARENTS. THEY COULD DETAIN ME FOR HOURS, OR FOR DAYS. I COULD BE WHIPPED. IN SHORT, ANYTHING COULD HAPPEN TO ME. IT WAS TIME FOR ACTION.

I'M SORRY MA'AM! I'LL NEVER DO IT AGAIN...

GET IN THE CAR!

MA'AM, MY MOTHER'S DEAD. MY STEPMOTHER IS REALLY CRUEL AND IF I DON'T GO HOME RIGHT AWAY, SHE'LL KILL ME...

SHE'LL BURN ME WITH THE CLOTHES IRON!

SHE'LL MAKE MY FATHER PUT ME IN AN ORPHANAGE.

MAYBE SHE BELIEVED ME, MAYBE SHE JUST PRETENDED TO. BUT, MIRACULOUSLY, SHE LET ME GO

BACK HOME...

MARJI! WHAT HAPPENED? HAVE YOU BEEN CRYING?

NO MOM, I'M JUST TIRED. I'M GOING TO MY ROOM.

THERE WAS NO WAY I COULD TELL THE TRUTH. SHE NEVER WOULD HAVE LET ME GO OUT ALONE AGAIN.

I GOT OFF PRETTY EASY, CONSIDERING. THE GUARDIANS OF THE REVOLUTION DIDN'T FIND MY TAPES.

♫ WE'RE THE KIDS IN AMERICA WHOAO ♫

TO EACH HIS OWN WAY OF CALMING DOW

THE SHABBAT

TO KEEP US FROM FORGETTING THAT WE WERE AT WAR, IRAQ OPTED FOR A NEW STRATEGY...

I HEARD THEY'RE GOING TO USE BALLISTIC MISSILES AGAINST US.

WHAT ARE YOU SAYING? WE'RE NOT AT WAR WITH THE SOVIET UNION. I DON'T BELIEVE THE IRAQIS HAVE WEAPONS LIKE THAT.

FROM THE IRAQI BORDER TO TEHRAN IT'S THOUSANDS OF MILES. MISSILES THAT CAN GO THAT FAR COST A FORTUNE!

WELL, THAT'S WHAT THE RUMORS SAY!

WE IRANIANS ARE OLYMPIC CHAMPIONS WHEN IT COMES TO GOSSIP.

SHE'S RIGHT. WE LOVE TO EXAGGERATE.

YOU SEEM TO HAVE THE OPPOSITE SYMPTOM.

WHY DO YOU SAY THAT?

EVEN WHEN YOU SEE SOMETHING WITH YOUR OWN EYES, YOU NEED CONFIRMATION FROM THE BBC.

MY NATURAL OPTIMISM JUST LEADS ME TO BE SKEPTICAL.

MOM'S PESSIMISM SOON WON OUT OVER DAD'S OPTIMISM. IT TURNED OUT THAT THE IRAQIS DID HAVE MISSILES. THEY WERE CALLED "SCUDS" AND TEHRAN BECAME THEIR TARGET.

WHEN THE SIRENS WENT ON, IT MEANT WE HAD THREE MINUTES TO KNOW IF THE END HAD COME.

WE'RE NOT GOING TO THE BASEMENT?

IT WOULDN'T MAKE ANY DIFFERENCE!!

CONSIDERING THE DAMAGE THEY DO, WHETHER WE'RE IN THE BASEMENT OR ON THE ROOF, IT'S THE SAME THING.

THE THREE MINUTES SEEMED LIKE THREE DAYS. FOR THE FIRST TIME, I REALIZED JUST HOW MUCH DANGER WE WERE IN.

BOOM!!

I DON'T WANT TO DIE!

YOU WON'T DEAR. I PROMISE YOU!

NOW THAT TEHRAN WAS UNDER ATTACK, MANY FLED. THE CITY WAS DESERTED. AS FOR US, WE STAYED. NOT JUST OUT OF FATALISM. IF THERE WAS TO BE A FUTURE, IN MY PARENTS' EYES, THAT FUTURE WAS LINKED TO MY FRENCH EDUCATION. AND TEHRAN WAS THE ONLY PLACE I COULD GET IT.

SOME PEOPLE, MORE CIRCUMSPECT, TOOK SHELTER IN THE BASEMENTS OF BIG HOTELS, WELL-KNOWN FOR THEIR SAFETY. APPARENTLY, THEIR REINFORCED CONCRETE STRUCTURES WERE BOMBPROOF.

ONE EXAMPLE WAS OUR NEIGHBORS, THE BABA-LEVYS. THEY WERE AMONG THE FEW JEWISH FAMILIES THAT HAD STAYED AFTER THE REVOLUTION. MR. BABA-LEVY SAID THEIR ANCESTORS HAD COME THREE THOUSAND YEARS AGO, AND IRAN WAS THEIR HOME.

...THEIR DAUGHTER NEDA WAS A QUIET GIRL WHO DIDN'T PLAY MUCH, BUT WE WOULD TALK ABOUT ROMANCE FROM TIME TO TIME.

...ONE DAY A BLOND PRINCE WITH BLUE EYES WILL COME AND TAKE ME TO HIS CASTLE...

OH YEAH! ME TOO!

SO LIFE WENT ON...

...ON ONE DAY, LIKE ANY OTHER:

MOM, CAN I HAVE SOME MONEY? I WANT TO GET SOME JEANS AND ESPADRILLES.

HOW MUCH?

OH, 1000, 1200 TUMANS.

1000 TUMANS?

YEP, THAT'S HOW MUCH THEY COST.

I SEE.

OUR CURRENCY HAD LOST ALL ITS VALUE. IT WAS SEVEN TUMANS TO THE DOLLAR WHEN THE SHAH WAS STILL AROUND. FOUR YEARS LATER IT WAS 110 TUMANS TO THE DOLLAR FOR MY MOTHER, THE CHANGE WAS SO SUDDEN THAT SHE HAD A HARD TIME ACCEPTING IT.

I WENT WITH MY FRIEND SHADI.

SO, HOW DO THEY LOOK?

THEY LOOK SUPER!

OK, I'LL TAKE THE JEANS, AND THESE EARRINGS.

AND I'LL TAKE THAT RING, THERE!

WE WERE IN THE MIDST OF SHOPPING EUPHORIA, WHEN SUDDENLY...

BOOM!!!

A MISSILE HAS JUST EXPLODED IN THE TAVANIR NEIGHBORHOOD.

WHAT!

TAVANIR WAS WHERE I LIVED.

پاراديزو

THE JEANS!

IF SOMEONE HAD TIMED ME, I THINK I WOULD HAVE BEAT THE WORLD SPEED RECORD.

TAXI!

FASTER! PLEASE HURRY...

A CROWD HAD GATHERED IN FRONT OF MY STREET! THE BOMB HAD HIT MY STREET!

MA'AM, WHICH BUILDING WAS HIT?

APPARENTLY, IT EXPLODED AT THE END OF THE STREET.

MY BUILDING AND THE BABA-EVY'S WERE AT THE END OF THE STREET.

LET ME THROUGH.

ONE CHANCE IN TWO THAT IT WAS OUR BUILDING.

PLEASE, LET ME THROUGH.

YOU CAN'T GO BEYOND THIS POINT!

...I LIVE HERE...

AND HE LET ME THROUGH.

I DIDN'T WANT TO LOOK UP. I LOOKED AT MY TREMBLING LEGS. I COULDN'T GO FORWARD, LIKE IN A NIGHTMARE.

LET THEM BE ALIVE. LET THEM BE ALIVE. LET THEM...

MARJI

MARJI!

MOM!

YOU'RE ALL RIGHT? DAD'S ALL RIGHT? GRANDMA'S ALL RIGHT?

EVERYONE'S OK. I WAS THE ONLY ONE HOME.

OH, MOM.

...

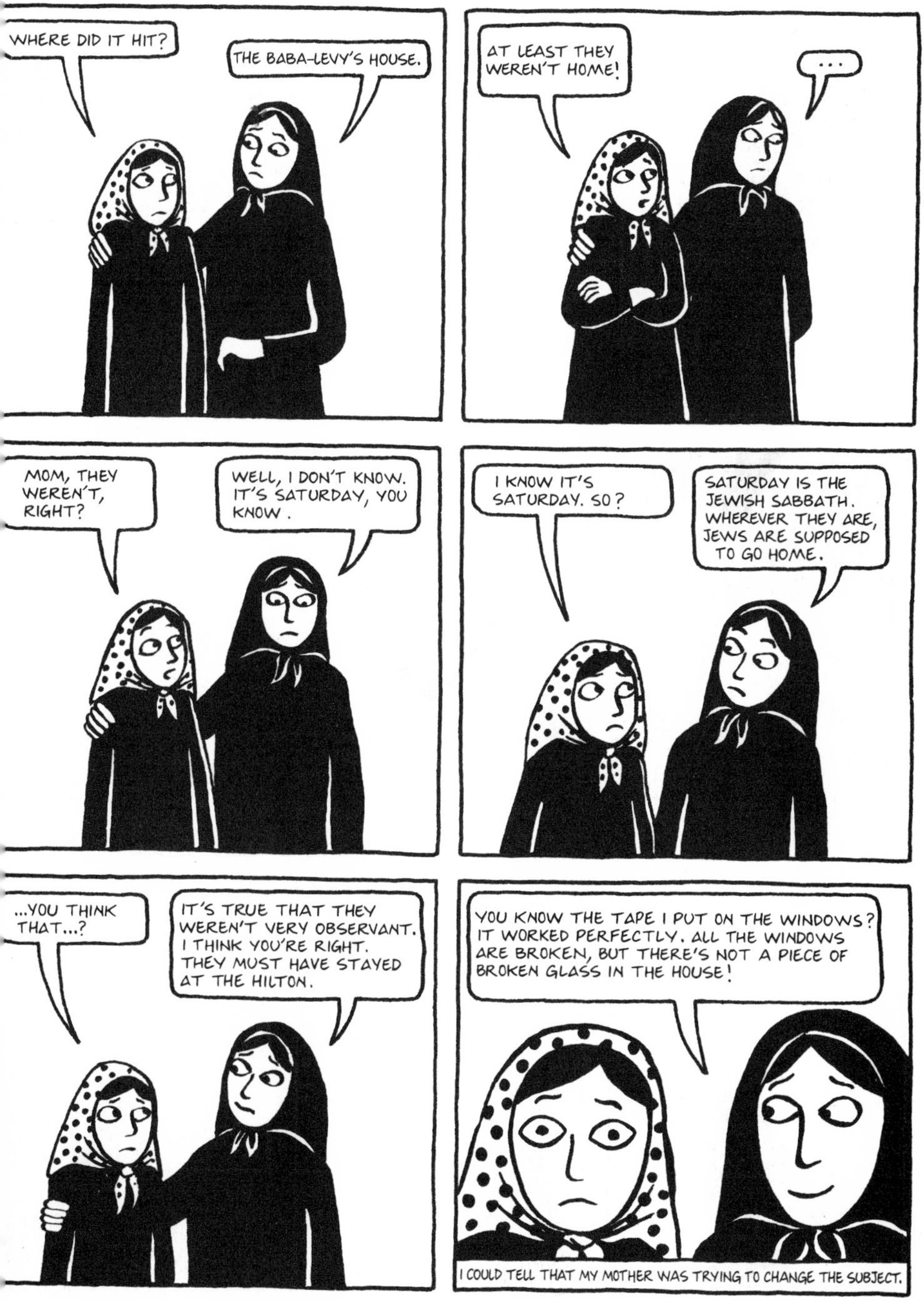
WHERE DID IT HIT?
THE BABA-LEVY'S HOUSE.
AT LEAST THEY WEREN'T HOME!
...
MOM, THEY WEREN'T, RIGHT?
WELL, I DON'T KNOW. IT'S SATURDAY, YOU KNOW .
I KNOW IT'S SATURDAY. SO?
SATURDAY IS THE JEWISH SABBATH. WHEREVER THEY ARE, JEWS ARE SUPPOSED TO GO HOME.
...YOU THINK THAT...?
IT'S TRUE THAT THEY WEREN'T VERY OBSERVANT. I THINK YOU'RE RIGHT. THEY MUST HAVE STAYED AT THE HILTON.
YOU KNOW THE TAPE I PUT ON THE WINDOWS? IT WORKED PERFECTLY. ALL THE WINDOWS ARE BROKEN, BUT THERE'S NOT A PIECE OF BROKEN GLASS IN THE HOUSE!
I COULD TELL THAT MY MOTHER WAS TRYING TO CHANGE THE SUBJECT.

WHEN WE WALKED PAST THE BABA-LEVY'S HOUSE, WHICH WAS COMPLETELY DESTROYED, I COULD FEEL THAT SHE WAS DISCREETLY PULLING ME AWAY. SOMETHING TOLD ME THAT THE BABA-LEVYS HAD BEEN AT HOME. SOMETHING CAUGHT MY ATTENTION.

I SAW A TURQUOISE BRACELET. IT WAS NEDA'S. HER AUNT HAD GIVEN IT TO HER FOR HER FOURTEENTH BIRTHDAY...

THE BRACELET WAS STILL ATTACHED TO... I DON'T KNOW WHAT...

NO SCREAM IN THE WORLD COULD HAVE RELIEVED MY SUFFERING AND MY ANGER.

THE DOWRY

AFTER THE DEATH OF NEDA BABA-LEVY, MY LIFE TOOK A NEW TURN. IN 1984, I WAS FOURTEEN AND A REBEL. NOTHING SCARED ME ANYMORE.

I'VE TOLD YOU A HUNDRED TIMES THAT IT IS STRICTLY FORBIDDEN TO WEAR JEWELRY AND JEANS!

WHAT ARE YOU DOING WITH THAT BRACELET? GIVE IT TO ME RIGHT NOW!

OVER MY DEAD BODY! IT WAS A GIFT FROM MY MOM.

HAD LEARNED THAT YOU SHOULD ALWAYS SHOUT LOUDER THAN YOUR AGGRESSOR.

IF YOU'RE STILL WEARING JEWELRY TOMORROW...

YEAH, I KNOW!

AND THE NEXT DAY...

LET ME SEE YOUR WRIST.

WHAT FOR?

LET ME SEE IT, I'M TELLING YOU.

WITH ALL THE JEWELRY YOU STEAL FROM US, YOU MUST BE MAKING A PILE OF MONEY.

WHAT HAPPENED?

MARJI HIT THE PRINCIPAL

SHE'S FINISHED!

EXCUSE ME! I DIDN'T MEAN IT!

SATRAPI, YOU'RE EXPELLED!

AFTER I WAS EXPELLED, IT WAS A REAL STRUGGLE TO FIND ANOTHER
SCHOOL THAT WOULD ACCEPT ME. HITTING THE PRINCIPAL WAS A
VERITABLE CRIME. BUT THANKS TO MY AUNT, WHO KNEW SOME
BUREAUCRATS IN THE EDUCATION SYSTEM, THEY MANAGED TO
PLACE ME IN ANOTHER SCHOOL. AND THERE...

SINCE THE ISLAMIC REPUBLIC WAS
FOUNDED, WE NO LONGER HAVE
POLITICAL PRISONERS.

MA'AM!

MY UNCLE WAS IMPRISONED BY THE SHAH'S
REGIME, BUT IT WAS THE ISLAMIC REGIME
THAT ORDERED HIS EXECUTION.

YOU SAY THAT WE DON'T
HAVE POLITICAL PRISONERS
ANYMORE. BUT WE'VE
GONE FROM 3000
PRISONERS UNDER THE
SHAH TO 300,000 UNDER
YOUR REGIME.

HOW DARE YOU LIE TO
US LIKE THAT?

OH, SATRAPI!

CLAP!
CLAP!
CLAP!
CLAP!
CLAP!
CLAP!
CLAP!
CLAP!
CLAP!

OBVIOUSLY, THAT EVENING MY FATHER GOT A PHONE CALL.

YES, OF COURSE...YES...

WHO IS IT?

IT WAS THE PRINCIPAL OF MARJI'S SCHOOL. APPARENTLY SHE TOLD OFF THE RELIGION TEACHER. SHE GETS THAT FROM HER UNCLE.

MAYBE YOU'D LIKE HER TO END UP LIKE HIM TOO? EXECUTED?

YOU KNOW WHAT THEY DO TO THE YOUNG GIRLS THEY ARREST?

YOU KNOW WHAT HAPPENED TO NILOUFAR? THE GIRL YOU MET AT KHOSRO'S HOUSE? THE MAN WHO MADE PASSPORTS?

YOU KNOW THAT IT'S AGAINST THE LAW TO KILL A VIRGIN...

SO A GUARDIAN OF THE REVOLUTION MARRIES HER...

...AND TAKES HER VIRGINITY BEFORE EXECUTING HER. DO YOU UNDERSTAND WHAT THAT MEANS???

IF SOMEONE SO MUCH AS TOUCHES A HAIR ON YOUR HEAD, I'LL KILL HIM!

BUT HOW DO YOU KNOW THAT FOR SURE? MAYBE THEY JUST EXECUTED HER!

NO. YOUR MOTHER'S RIGHT. TRADITIONALLY, WHEN A GIRL GETS MARRIED, THE HUSBAND IS SUPPOSED TO PAY HER A DOWRY.

IF THE GIRL DIES, THE HUSBAND HAS TO GIVE THE DOWRY TO HER FAMILY.

THAT'S WHAT HAPPENED WITH NILOUFAR. AFTER SHE WAS EXECUTED, TO MAKE SURE HER AWFUL FATE WAS UNDERSTOOD, THEY SENT 500 TUMANS* TO HER PARENTS.

500 TUMANS FOR THE LIFE AND VIRGINITY OF AN INNOCENT GIRL.

I HAD NO IDEA.

*EQUIVALENT TO $5.00

ALL NIGHT LONG, I THOUGHT OF THAT PHRASE: "TO DIE A MARTYR IS TO INJECT BLOOD INTO THE VEINS OF SOCIETY." NILOUFAR WAS A REAL MARTYR, AND HER BLOOD CERTAINLY DID NOT FEED OUR SOCIETY'S VEINS.

ONE WEEK LATER...

MARJI, CAN YOU COME HERE FOR A FEW MINUTES? WE WANT TO TALK TO YOU.

I WENT TO SEE THE PRINCIPAL TODAY. SHE ASSURED ME THAT SHE HAD NOT SENT A REPORT THIS TIME. BUT CONSIDERING THE PERSON YOU ARE AND THE EDUCATION YOU'VE RECEIVED, WE THOUGHT THAT IT WOULD BE BETTER IF YOU LEFT IRAN.

WHAT?

YOUR MOTHER AND I HAVE DECIDED TO SEND YOU TO AUSTRIA.

WHY AUSTRIA?

FIRST OF ALL, BECAUSE IT'S EASIER TO GET AN AUSTRIAN VISA, AND SECOND BECAUSE MY BEST FRIEND LIVES IN VIENNA. DO YOU REMEMBER HER? ZOZO? SHERINE'S MOM?

YEAH, YEAH. BUT I DON'T SPEAK GERMAN!

THERE'S A FRENCH SCHOOL IN VIENNA. ONE OF THE BEST IN EUROPE!

AND WHAT ARE YOU GOING TO DO THERE?

YOU'RE GOING ON AHEAD OF US. WE HAVE SOME BUSINESS TO TAKE CARE OF. WE'LL JOIN YOU A FEW MONTHS FROM NOW!

BUT I'M ONLY FOURTEEN! YOU TRUST ME?

YOU'RE FOURTEEN AND I KNOW HOW I BROUGHT YOU UP. ABOVE ALL, I TRUST YOUR EDUCATION.

YOU'RE THE SAME PERSON WHO WENT ON VACATION TO FRANCE ALL BY YOURSELF, REMEMBER?

BEFORE THE REVOLUTION, MY PARENTS SENT ME TO SUMMER CAMP IN FRANCE. MY MOTHER DIDN'T WANT ME TO GROW UP LIKE AN ONLY CHILD.

IT'S TRUE, THAT WAS GREAT...REAL INDEPENDENCE.

WE LOVE YOU SO MUCH THAT WE WANT YOU TO GO.

WE FEEL IT'S BETTER FOR YOU TO BE FAR AWAY AND HAPPY THAN CLOSE BY AND MISERABLE. JUDGING BY THE SITUATION HERE, YOU'LL BE BETTER OFF SOMEWHERE ELSE.

AT THAT POINT, I STARTED TO HAVE MY DOUBTS. WHY SAY THOSE THINGS IF THEY WERE COMING TOO?

WE ADORE YOU!

DON'T EVER FORGET WHO YOU ARE!

NO. I WON'T EVER FORGET.

I REPEATED WHAT THEY HAD TOLD ME OVER AND OVER IN MY HEAD. I WAS PRETTY SURE THEY WEREN'T COMING TO VIENNA.

I STAYED UP ALL NIGHT AND WONDERED IF THE MOON SHONE AS BRIGHTLY IN VIENNA.

THE NEXT DAY I FILLED A JAR WITH SOIL FROM OUR GARDEN. IRANIAN SOIL.

I TOOK DOWN ALL OF MY POSTERS.

KIM WI

I INVITED MY GIRLFRIENDS OVER TO SAY GOODBYE.

HERE. I'M GIVING YOU MY MOST PRECIOUS THINGS, SO THAT YOU WON'T FORGET ME.

I NEVER REALIZED HOW MUCH THEY LOVED ME.

AND I UNDERSTOOD HOW IMPORTANT THEY WERE TO ME.

ON THE EVE OF MY DEPARTURE, MY GRANDMOTHER CAME TO SPEND THE NIGHT AT OUR HOUSE.

CAN I SLEEP WITH YOU?

THAT'S WHY I'M HERE!

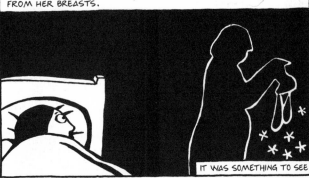

I WATCHED MY GRANDMA UNDRESS. EACH MORNING, SHE PICKED JASMINE FLOWERS TO PUT IN HER BRA SO THAT SHE WOULD SMELL NICE. WHEN SHE UNDRESSED, YOU COULD SEE THE FLOWERS FALL FROM HER BREASTS.

IT WAS SOMETHING TO SEE

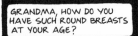

GRANDMA, HOW DO YOU HAVE SUCH ROUND BREASTS AT YOUR AGE?

EVERY MORNING AND NIGHT, I SOAK THEM IN A BOWL OF ICE WATER FOR TEN MINUTES.

SHE ACTUALLY DID, AND I KNEW IT. I JUST WANTED TO HEAR HER SAY IT.

I'LL MISS YOU.

OH, I'LL COME SEE YOU.

SHE TOO WAS LYING TO ME.

LISTEN, I DON'T WANT TO PREACH, BUT LET ME GIVE YOU SOME ADVICE THAT WILL ALWAYS HELP YOU.

IN LIFE YOU'LL MEET A LOT OF JERKS. IF THEY HURT YOU, TELL YOURSELF THAT IT'S BECAUSE THEY'RE STUPID. THAT WILL HELP KEEP YOU FROM REACTING TO THEIR CRUELTY. BECAUSE THERE IS NOTHING WORSE THAN BITTERNESS AND VENGEANCE... ALWAYS KEEP YOUR DIGNITY AND BE TRUE TO YOURSELF.

I SMELLED MY GRANDMA'S BOSOM. IT SMELLED GOOD. I'LL NEVER FORGET THAT SMELL.

AND THE NEXT MORNING.

WAKE UP! IT'S SEVEN O'CLOCK. WE'VE GOT TO GO.

?

I WILL ALWAYS BE TRUE TO MYSELF.

I'M NOT COMING ALONG.

DON'T EVER FORGET WHAT I TOLD YOU.

GRANDMA

HERE WE ARE!

THERE WAS A HUGE LINE. LOTS OF PEOPLE WERE LEAVING THE COUNTRY.

ESPECIALLY YOUNG BOYS, CONSIDERED FUTURE SOLDIERS, THEY WERE FORBIDDEN TO LEAVE THE COUNTRY AFTER THEY TURNED THIRTEEN.

MEHRABAD AIRPORT

WHAT I HAD FEARED WAS TRUE. MAYBE THEY'D COME TO VISIT, BUT WE'D NEVER LIVE TOGETHER AGAIN.

I COULDN'T BEAR LOOKING AT THEM THERE BEHIND THE GLASS.
NOTHING'S WORSE THAN SAYING GOODBYE. IT'S A LITTLE LIKE DYING.

GO ON,
GO ON.

CLOSE YOUR
SUITCASE,
YOU CAN GO.

I COULDN'T JUST GO...

I TURNED AROUND TO SEE THEM
ONE LAST TIME.

IT WOULD HAVE BEEN BETTER TO JUST GO.

CREDITS

Translation of first part: Mattias Ripa
Translation of second part: Blake Ferris
Supervision of translation: Marjane Satrapi and Carol Bernstein
Lettering: Eve Deluze
Additional hand lettering: Céline Merrien

THANKS TO

Anjali Singh
L'Association
David B.
Jean-Christophe Menu
Emile Bravo
Christophe Blain
Guillaume Dumora
Fanny Dalle-Rive
Nicolas Leroy
Matthieu Wahiche
Charlotte Miquel